# Accreditation Helps

# Accreditation Helps

An Introduction to the Theology of the
Christian and Missionary Alliance

## Ben Elliott

*WingSpread Publishers*

Chicago, Illinois

*WingSpread Publishers*
*Chicago, Illinois*

www.moodypublishers.com

*An imprint of Moody Publishers*

Library and Archives Canada Cataloguing in Publication

CIP data on file with the National Library and Archives
ISBN: 978-1-60066337-6
benjamin.c.elliott@gmail.com

Scripture quotations are taken from the Holy Bible, New Living Translation, copyright © 1996. Used by permission of Tyndale House Publishers, Inc., Wheaton, Illinois 60189. All rights reserved.

Cover design by Curtis Mulder.

5 7 9 10 8 6

Printed in the United States of America

To order additional copies, please call e-church depot at 800.233.4443.

# Contents

# Introduction

These are not the answers to the Alliance's doctrinal questionnaire, or to questions from the accreditation or ordination interview. In fact, these are not even the questions. The goal of this book is not to present a series of questions and answers to be memorized by accreditation candidates, but rather to create a framework for discussing the most important issues in Alliance dogmatics, especially for the use of candidates and mentors (and perhaps the examination team too might find something of use), as they prepare for accreditation or ordination within the Christian and Missionary Alliance.

Although candidates are often eager for materials to help them prepare for accreditation, very little is available, even less from a specifically Alliance perspective; the most recent systematic treatment of Alliance thought, for example, was written before the First World War and speaks to current readers only from a great distance. It is my hope in writing that I can help to address this lack. These are not *the* answers, but this book genuinely is a part of the conversation that we need to be having.

The following, then, are the questions that I would ask as an accreditation mentor or examiner, and alongside them are the answers I myself would give. This book is not intended as an exhaustive systematic theology, but it has been written systematically, and I am confident that the candidate who has worked through the questions with his or her mentor or cohort group—and who understands the fundamental issues addressed by them—stands well prepared for whatever may come in the theology section of their interview. All God's best to you,

Benjamin Elliott
Jakarta, Indonesia, 2012

# 1. The Christian Faith

*Which two or three Bible verses sum up your understanding of the Christian faith? Why?*

For me, there are three verses that stand at the center of Christian theology. I don't by any stretch mean that these are the only three choices; A. B. Simpson, the founder of the Alliance, might be happier if I chose Colossians 1:27 and Matthew 24:14. The important thing is that before you come to your accreditation interview you have taken the time to think through what it actually means to be a Christian—and to be a Christian minister—and that your explanation is an explanation that comes from the Bible. So, for myself, if I had to pick out verses to sum up what Christianity means, these would be my top three.

The distinguishing mark of Christianity is this: we believe that when you look at Jesus, you see God himself at work: not a messenger from God, nor a project that God is putting into action, but actually God, coming to save us. Sin had created this irreparable rift between God and humanity, and God, rather than waiting for us to come and meet him halfway, bridged the whole gap in Jesus Christ, not counting our sins against us, and created anew the relationship that we had destroyed. And now, he has committed this message of reconciliation to us, meaning not only that we are responsible for communicating this message to the world—the message that it was God who was in Christ, reconciling us to himself—but also that we are responsible to ourselves be God's agents of reconciliation, people who by the power of God the Holy Spirit work to create restored relationships in the world. This is what the Holy Spirit teaches us through Paul in 2 Corinthians 5:19, that "God was in Christ, reconciling the world to himself, no longer counting people's sins against them. And he gave us this wonderful message of reconciliation."

Nothing can stand in the way of God accomplishing his plan, and his plan is this: that he would freely share his love with us, and that we would receive it and would freely love him back. The fact that God accomplishes this plan displays his might; the fact that he does it without compromising displays his holiness. But the plan itself—a plan he made before the creation of the world—tells us something about who he is. He is so full of love that it overflows: the Father loves the Son so super-abundantly that God makes a plan to create, just so that there are creatures who can receive his love and respond to it. He is unsatisfied sharing his love just a little, and so he chooses to create human beings, creatures who share his own image and are capable of genuinely responding to his love. When they choose to reject him, he woos them and makes possible their return; when they return he makes possible their love and calls them his sons and daughters. This is not something he pieces together as he goes along, it has always been his plan: to share the loving life of who he is as Father, Son, and Holy Spirit, so that the Son would stand as the firstborn in the midst of a joyous, large family. This is the message of Romans 8:29, that "God knew his people in advance, and he chose them to become like his Son, so that his Son would be the firstborn among many brothers and sisters."

For many, God seems hard to see. To be sure, God is always far above us, in the fullest sense of the word above. Nothing we can do can reach up to or around him, or control even the idea of him with our minds. But although we cannot corral God intellectually, we can know him. An idea is something that you know about; a person is someone you can know. God is not an idea that we can comprehend with our brains, he much bigger and much different than that. We know God in the kind of way that we know another person, because persons, created in the image of God, are in this way the same kind of thing that God is. We come to know God personally—like a person—not because we have somehow grabbed hold of him like an idea, but because he expresses himself in such a way as to be knowable by us. He doesn't push his way into our lives; if we do not wish to know him, he does not force himself upon us. But if we seek hard for him, he promises that we will be able to find him. Seeing him is the reward of seeking him. Before, however, we can seek him, we must believe that he exists. Apologetics are not something that can prove the existence of God; their usefulness is in pointing to the fact that belief in God is a reasonable stance, likely the most reasonable. But for us to know God, we must decide ahead of time to accept that he exists, which always remains an act of faith. Christianity can never be proven, it is always based on faith in the Person and saving act of Jesus Christ. This guarantees that when we love God back, our love has never been forced, which is important because forced love is not real love. And so, Hebrews 11:6 says that "it is impossible to please God without faith. Anyone who wants to come to him must believe that God exists and that he rewards those who sincerely seek him."

### *If I was preparing for accreditation I would . . .*

- Take the time to think through what Christianity means to me, and be prepared to share about it
- Double check that I had memorized my favorite Bible verses, and think through how I would explain why they are important to me

# 2. The Trinity

## *What does it mean that God is Triune?*

The word 'Trinity' is not a word that comes from the Bible. It is, however, a word that is packed with Biblical content. It is a word that was invented by the Church to try and sum up as carefully as possible who God had revealed himself to be, as recorded in the Scriptures. And so, because it has the weight of both the Bible and the early Church standing so strongly behind it, we use the word 'Trinity' as a primary way of talking about God, and we use the concept of 'God as Triune' as the key to understanding Christian theology.

There are two critical halves to understanding the doctrine of the Trinity. The first half is the confession that God is the one and only God. From the opening verses of the Old Testament, it is God and God alone who rules over everything, and it is God who creates out of nothing. He is not pictured as the strongest among the rest of the gods—he is in fact the only thing that exists at all, except for the things he freely chooses to create. This theme that there is only one true God runs through the whole of God's revelation to us. Isaiah prophecies: "This is what the LORD says—Israel's King and Redeemer, the LORD of Heaven's Armies: 'I am the First and the Last; there is no other God.'" (Is 44:6) Paul writes in Romans 3:30 that "there is only one God, and he makes people right with himself only by faith, whether they are Jews or Gentiles."

In theological language, when we want to describe this fact that there is only one God, we say that 'God is one substance' or, using the Greek technical term for God's substance, that 'God is one *ousia*'. To emphasize that this *substance* or *ousia* is not some kind of stuff that God is made out of, you could also just plainly say that 'God is one God'; the key thing to remember is that this half of the definition of the Trinity simply communicates the Scriptural confession that God is the only God, and he cannot be added to or broken into smaller pieces: there is no other.

The second half of understanding the Trinity is the confession 'Jesus is Lord' that we find dozens of times in various forms throughout the New Testament, a radical break from the Judaism the disciples had grown up with and a reflection of Jesus' own life and teaching. One of the chief reasons why the Jewish leaders were so inflamed toward Jesus was the fact that "he not only broke the Sabbath, he called God his Father, thereby making himself equal with God." (Jn 5:18) In John 10:30, Jesus openly says "The Father and I are one," and the Jews prepare to stone him on the spot for blasphemy. More privately, Jesus counsels his fearful disciples at the last supper that "anyone who has seen me has seen the Father." (Jn 14:9) So then, following the resurrection of Jesus and the coming of the Holy Spirit when their understanding was made complete, the disciples did not hesitate to declare to the world that Jesus was indeed the "Lord of all" (Ac 10:36) and "our great God and Savior." (2P 1:1)

These two halves, then, form the foundation of the doctrine of the Trinity: God is one God, and Jesus is Lord. But how? How can the Father be God, and the Son be God, and God be one? Going even further, we find in both the Scripture and in the earliest Church, alongside the discussion of the divinity of Jesus, an equivalent and parallel discussion of the deity of the Holy Spirit and his relationship to the Father. Just as Jesus was recognized to be fully God, so was the Holy Spirit in every way, an equal of Father and Son. (See Mt 28:19, 2Co 13:14) When I consider each one, I confess that Father, Son, and Spirit are each God; when I consider God, I confess that he is the one and only God.

The word used by the Church to describe the Father, the Son, and the Holy Spirit—when we consider them individually—is 'Person', or *'hypostasis'*. And, from the very first, the Church has confessed all three of these as Persons of the Godhead: fully divine, fully equal, distinguishable one from another as we see them at work in the world, but participating together. The question of exactly how these three Persons could each be fully God and yet God be one God was not a question that troubled the early Church; they were so totally convinced that both of the foundational halves of the definition were true that they were by and large unconcerned with explaining exactly how they fit together. Thus, the most basic description of God as Triune—the one that we use even today (and that you should memorize before your accreditation exam)—is simply a statement of the facts rather than an explanation: 'God is three Persons, one substance', or 'one *ousia*, three *hypostasis*'.

The term 'Trinity', then, and all the discussion that surrounds it, is the result of the Church's struggle to explain this reality more precisely, especially in the face of a series of heresies (false teachings) that emphasized either the one-ness of God or the deity of Jesus by marginalizing the importance of the other theme. The doctrine of the Trinity, then, is not a precise definition like Peano's axioms, but a set of four boundaries that keep us from wandering off when we talk about God (I kind of imagine it like a big box). There is a lot of space inside this box to continue exploring who God is and who he is to me, and we can explore that space safely because the walls of the box protect us from going too far afield. Conversely, when we come across Trinitarian ideas that are 'outside the box', we are able to quickly identify them and protect ourselves and those to whom we minister from being led astray. The doctrine of the Trinity can be defined in this way by describing the following four boundaries (or 'walls' of the box).

First, the Father, the Son, and the Holy Spirit are distinguishable from one another. The Father is God, the Son is God, and the Holy Spirit is God; but the Son is not the Father, nor is the Father the Spirit, nor the Spirit the Son. Remember that the Trinity is simply a doctrine that is trying to express in words how God has revealed himself. God has shown himself to be a Father, who sends his Son, who in turn is accompanied by and gives the Holy Spirit. We distinguish between Father, Son, Spirit because the Bible itself distinguishes between them; we acknowledge each one as a fully divine Person because the Bible shows them interacting together (which is why we cannot think of them merely as the one God merely appearing in different ways on different occasions, as in the heresy of 'Modalism'; see Mt 3:16-17) and treating one another as distinguishable divine Persons. (Jn

14:16, 2P 1:17) We never see them collapsed into or explained away by the presence of another. Each member of the Trinity is both genuinely divine and genuinely personal—meaning they are like a person—none is simply a *force* or an *it* (we use the pronouns 'he' and 'his' in reference to the Persons of the Trinity not because they are male but because they are *personal*, and 'he' is the most neutral personal pronoun we have in English; the word 'it' cannot be used of the Persons of the Trinity any more than it can be used of any other person). In formal theological discussion, the word 'distinguishable' is usually used when talking about the 'three-ness' of the Persons of the Trinity—rather than words like 'distinct' or 'individual' or 'separate'—to help us always keep in mind that Father, Son, and Holy Spirit are not three different gods but the one and only God, expressed in three Persons. The Father is God, the Son is God, the Holy Spirit is God, but you can distinguish between them. Any doctrine of God that fails to thus distinguish between the three divine Persons must be counted as incorrect.

Second, God is *one*; although Father, Son, and Spirit are distinguishable from one another, there is only one God. However we describe God, we cannot even for a moment allow ourselves to consider that he could be broken into pieces or in any way duplicated. He, and only he, is the one, indivisible, un-reproducible God. This is what we mean when we say that God is one substance. Even though it can be difficult to describe in words just exactly how to understand the relationship between the 'three-ness' of the Persons and the 'one-ness' of the substance of God, we never back down from our confession that there is, and can only be, one God.

God *is* three Persons, but he *is* nevertheless one substance, and any doctrine of God that fails to assert this full unity (or 'one-ness') of God is incorrect.

Third, the primary way for us to understand the 'three-in-one-ness' of God is by looking at the Father, Son, and Holy Spirit in relationship together. 1 John 4:16 says that "God is love," that is, the very essence, or substance (the *ousia*), of God *is* love. Extending through all eternity, the Father has a relationship of superabundant love with the Son, and the Son with the Spirit, and the Spirit with the Father: Father, Son, and Spirit, sharing a perfect love. The unity of God— the one undivided substance that God is—is this love, this relationship. Only together, only loving, do the members of the Trinity mutually make one another who they are as the one God. The substance of God is relational substance, not something that can be comprehended apart from God himself, but rather the love itself which each divine Person equally gives to and receives from the others. The love *is* the substance. God is not merely a God who loves, he is the God who *is* love, whose very being consists of the eternal love between Father, Son, and Holy Spirit. This is why it is not problematic for us to consider the unity of God to be the kind of unity that can allow for 'three-ness'. It is precisely on account of the Three that the One exists, because it is the Three who love. The technical term for this kind of unity, a unity of members who interpenetrate and contribute together to the reality of one another, is *'perichoresis'*. It means that the Father is the Father on account of his loving and being loved by the Son and the Spirit—on account of his being Father; it means that the one God is in his very essence indivisibly one with the kind of 'one-ness' that is sustained out of 'three-ness'. When we speak of '*perichoresis*', we mean that although we distinguish between the Persons when we think about them, we remember that each one is always present in the other, because each one is who he is only on account of the others—the relationship of the three *is* the substance of the one. And because the very essence of God is love, the divine persons are never lonely or alone (or in need of us humans for companionship). The *perichoretic* unity of God is a festive and loving unity; God's life is a vibrant and social life, not a solitary one. Even in the act of creation God says 'us'. (Gen 1:26, 3:22) So, while the longer answer of how the One are Three and the Three are One is slower to explain, the broad strokes can be made clear, God can be described by the word 'Trinity'—as the three-in-one—because God is love, and any doctrine of the Trinity which solves the problem of the 'one-ness' and 'three-ness' of God by pushing the love relationship between Father, Son, and Holy Spirit to the sidelines is incorrect.

Thus far: distinguishability, unity, and perichoretic love— the fourth fixed boundary of the doctrine of the Trinity is *equality*, the equality of the Persons. Spirit, Son, and Father are all equally God, each one equal in worth, equal in glory, equal in Personhood, equal in honor, equal in position, and equal in time. The Father is not before or above the Son and the Holy Spirit, nor is one more 'God' than another. You see, when we talk about the distinguishability of the divine Persons, it is often easiest to talk about what they do: the Father is the Creator and the Sender, the Son is the Redeemer and the Sent One, the Spirit is the Sanctifier and the Gift. This kind of language is totally appropriate (and Biblical), but when we think about God himself, it is more helpful to use relational terms to describe God rather than terms that are rooted in what he *does* for us. What I mean is this: I am in fact the 'reader' of bedtime stories and the 'payer' for my kids' food and clothes, but if you are really trying to describe who I am, I prefer to be thought of as 'dad', which says something about my personal identity, not just what I do. My worth to my kids is not contingent on my role in the family, it is connected to *who I am*, independent of what I do. And so, when we take the time to try and formally describe God, we differentiate the Father by speaking of him as the *unbegotten*, of the Son as the *only begotten*, and of the Holy Spirit as the one who *proceeds* from the Father and the Son. This is a reflection of the Biblical revelation of the Son as the one who is begotten of the Father (Jn 3:16), and of the Holy Spirit as proceeding from the Father and the Son (Jn 14:16, 20:22), of course not meaning that the Son is begotten in same the way as you or I. To be extra careful, especially to rule out the idea that in the very beginning the Father was alone, and then only later the Son and Spirit came into being (the Arian heresy), it can sometimes be helpful to use language like 'eternally begotten' or 'eternally proceeds'; distinguishing between the Persons does not lessen their equality, even when we refer to their very origin. Gregory of Nyssa, one of the great Christian bishops of the fourth century, said that the Trinity is like a family, like Adam, Eve, and Abel. Adam was not begotten, but formed by God from the dust of the earth, Eve was made from Adam, and Abel was begotten of them both. All are equal in nature—equally human, equally valuable—all of them in relationship together (and none of them on their own) make up that one family. Each one so very much the same, even though each one is different in origin and distinguishable in person. That is a little bit what God is like. The Triune Persons are not identical, but they *are* radically equal. Any doctrine of God that fails to assert this full equality of the Triune Persons, that stacks them up as higher or lower than one another in deity or glory, is incorrect.

God is one; Jesus is Lord. These are the two foundational facts of revelation that explain what Christians mean when they say that God is Triune, that he is simultaneously three Persons and one substance. Our understanding of his three-in-one-ness, although not exhaustive, is one bounded by the distinguishability, unity, love relationship, and complete equality of the divine Persons. Father, Son, and Holy Spirit are each fully God, each fully glorious and worthy of worship, and each fully personal in the truest sense of the word. So too, God is one mysterious God, whose 'one-ness' the Bible sums up with a single word: love.

### *If I was preparing for accreditation I would . . .*

- Be aware of the definition 'three Persons, one substance'
- Understand the meaning of the terms '*perichoresis*', '*hypostasis*', and '*ousia*'
- Understand the how the terms 'begotten' and 'proceeds' are used in regards to the Trinity
- Memorize Isaiah 44:6 and one of Matthew 3:16-17, Matthew 28:19, or 2 Corinthians 13:14
- Think about how passages that are already quite common to us, like John 3:16 or Titus 3:4-7, teach us about God as Triune

# 3. The Importance of the Trinity

*Why is the doctrine of the Trinity important?*

## The doctrine of the Trinity is true

Fundamentally, the doctrine of the Trinity is important because it is true. To say that 'God is three Persons, one substance' is not simply to recite a traditional sentence that our ancestors in the Church have found meaningful but we don't really understand, it is to speak something that is actually true about who God *is*, and who he has revealed himself to be. If we lose touch with the doctrine of the Trinity—or worse, start to think about God in some other way—we will have stopped thinking about God in the way he really is, having replaced him with some idea from our own human imaginations. If we abandon the Trinity we become like the people Paul wrote about who "traded the truth about God for a lie." (Ro 1:25)

Because it is true, the Trinity helps us to understand the rest of Christian theology: who God really is, and who we really are, created in his image. It is the key that allows us to make sense of the whole. For example, only when I have learned from the doctrine of the Trinity that the basic reality of God's being is love, can I understand how God the Son could empty himself of power and glory—the things we most often consider the most important bits of being God—and take the position of a slave . . . and yet still be God. (Php

2:6-8) The doctrine of the Trinity teaches me that Christ left behind the things that God *has*, but nothing of what it meant for him to truly *be* God: love.

Only having learned from the doctrine of the Trinity that the Sender and the Sent are radically equal—that differences in role are not the same as differences in value and worth—can I fully understand what God intended *my* family to be. I, and my wife, and our kids are all different, and all contribute to family life in different amounts and in different ways. And yet all are equally loved, equally worthwhile, and equally irreplaceable parts of the family regardless of *what we do*; I learn from the doctrine of the Trinity that my wife and I don't have to be identical to be equal (which is great, because we are not identical at all), but that *who we are* is somehow connected to our love for one another—to the way that we sacrifice ourselves one for the other—and to the way we let that love overflow to others. The doctrine of the Trinity is thus a trustworthy guide in helping us understand God and the world he has created. The Trinity is important because it is true.

## The doctrine of the Trinity is unique

Another reason why the Trinity is important, and important to understand clearly, is because of its place as a uniquely Christian doctrine. There are, of course, many similarities between Christianity and other world religions, but the doctrine of the Trinity is particular to the Church. This is important for two reasons. First, it gives us something in common with our Christian brothers and sisters around the world, even when we disagree with them about all sorts of other things. Paul writes of the Church that "we are many parts of one body, and we all belong to each other." (Ro 12:5) Yet although this is only one of many New Testament passages that teach about Christian unity, the reality in the Church is that we are divided. More than that, the fact of all our different denominations and groups makes it hard to imagine how the Church possibly *could* be reunited, even if we all wanted to. The Trinity, however, is one thing that we all still share, and provides us and our brother and sister Christians in other churches a little piece of common ground as a basis both for dialogue and for shared ministry in our cities and around the world. Our shared and unique understanding that God is Triune reminds us that although the Orthodox and the Catholics and the Quakers and all manner of others seem so strange and distant from us, fundamentally, they make up with us the whole body of Christ, and we can be encouraged—and challenged—in remembering that "we all belong to each other."

Second, the uniqueness of the doctrine of the Trinity clearly sets us apart from other world religions. Not so that we can boast of being different just for difference's sake, but because it is important to be able to clearly talk about exactly what it is that sets Christianity apart. In the country where I live, for example, Islam is by far the majority religion, and one of the most important questions we face—both inside the church and evangelistically—is whether God and Allah are the same, and if they are different, how? And what difference does it make? That conversation is impossible without really understanding what we mean when we say that God is both three and one. If we do not really understand the Trinity, we will never be able to clearly explain the differences between Christianity and its religious 'neighbors', either to our friends or to ourselves. The Trinity—this unique Christian doctrine—is important because it ties us together, and because it sets us apart.

## The doctrine of the Trinity is essential to the doctrine of salvation

Finally, and preeminently, the doctrine of the Trinity is important because it stands at the core of the gospel message: if there is no Trinity, there is no salvation. Remember that the Trinity is not an abstract concept, but simply a way of preserving in words the Biblical truth that 'God is the only God' and that 'Jesus is Lord'—that both assertions are equally and totally true—especially against opponents to Christian belief from Arius to Muhammad who have been unwilling to accept that Jesus is fully God, just as the Father is. This concept is so critical because only as Lord is Jesus also our savior.

You see, the core of the gospel is this: that helpless humanity, lost in sin, has been saved by God's mighty act to reach in and rescue, and to create anew in Jesus Christ. Salvation means more than repair; it means a genuinely new beginning in Christ. This is why the Bible says that "anyone who belongs to Christ has become a new person. The old life is gone; a new life has begun . . . for God was in Christ, reconciling the world to himself, no longer counting people's sins against them." (2Co 5:17, 19) Salvation this complete is something only God himself could accomplish. Only God himself could bear the full brunt of God's own wrath against our sins (1P 2:24), and pronounce the amnesty of God upon them (Mk 2:5-7); and who else but God alone could create a new reality, one where our relationship with God is healed and restored? (Col 1:16-20) This is why the Father did not send a prophet or an angel to save, he sent his Son, (Hb 1:1-13) because the problem of Sin cannot be resolved by a delegate, but only by the one who is able to create something good out of nothing, only by "our great God and Savior, Jesus Christ." (Ti 2:13)

And so, Paul writes in 1 Corinthians 15:17 that "if Christ has not been raised, then your faith is useless and you are still guilty of your sins." Paul understood that if there has been no resurrection, then there has been no salvation, because the resurrection is the sign that Jesus really is who he said he is, the very Son of God. If Christ did not rise again, then he isn't *really* the Lord, isn't *really* God himself with the power to save. If Christ did not rise again, then we haven't *really* been saved, haven't *really* been re-created. But he *did* rise again, and he *is* the Lord. The Bible says that "he was shown to be the Son of God when he was raised from the dead by the power of the Holy Spirit. He is Jesus Christ our Lord." (Ro 1:4) Our need, the need for *God himself* to come rescue us and give us new life, has been met in this Jesus, who is the Lord.

The actions of Jesus to save—his life, ministry, teaching, death, and resurrection—are the actions of God, and only as God is he truly our savior. This is why the Trinity is important. Only with the doctrine of the Trinity can we stand against the world and say both that 'God is one God' and that 'Jesus is Lord'. 'Trinity' is not some magic word that holds Christianity together, but it *is* a mighty word because it declares that Jesus, who claimed the divine right to save us and create us anew, in fact *has* that right, and we truly *are* saved because of him. Remember: the doctrine of the Trinity is just a careful way of saying that Jesus, along with the Holy Spirit, is distinguishable from the Father but is nevertheless God himself at work to reconcile mankind to himself. The Trinity is important because it preserves for us the center of the gospel, that our savior is Jesus Christ the Lord. (Lk 2:11, Php 3:20)

*If I was preparing for accreditation I would . . .*
- Think through why the doctrine of the Trinity is important for me
- Memorize 1 Corinthians 15:17

# 4. God's Character

*Describe the character of God*

What is God like? It's hard to say, isn't it. The Bible says that "no one has ever seen God. But the one and only Son is himself God and is near to the Father's heart. He has revealed God to us." (Jn 1:18) On our own, describing the character of God is impossible—even if we try to do it by taking all the best things in creation and in our imaginations and multiplying them as highly and nobly as we can—because *no one has ever seen God.* If we want to describe the character of God, our only choice is to begin with Jesus.

And Jesus teaches us that the best word to use when we talk about God is *Father*, because Jesus himself is the Son.

Talking about God then, fundamentally, is like talking about a person. For example, if I were asked to describe my wife, it would be bizarre for me to begin by saying that she is a human female, an earthbound member of the animal kingdom, bestowed with rationality and the capacity for relationship. Yet although we recognize how odd it would be to describe another human being like this, it is nevertheless easy for us to fall into the trap of talking about God in just the same way. Of course God *is* immortal, and omniscient, and perfect. But using those kinds of words is a strange way to *begin* the conversation about a personal God, especially one whose Spirit teaches our hearts to call him "Abba, Father." (Gal 4:6) The challenge of describing God is not one of cataloguing a series of traits and qualities that he possesses—even awesome ones—in the way that we would treat a plant or a star; it is much more like thinking through how you would respond to someone who asked: "Tell me what your mom is like."

As pastors and church leaders therefore, it is less important that we can address philosophical questions about the maximum-ness of God than that we can respond when people ask us: "Tell me what your God is like." And so, whenever we talk about God, we need to be vigilant not to cave to the pressure of discussing *what* he is, rather than *who* he is, because *who* he is—and who he is for us—is ultimately what counts.

For me, the answer to the question of *what is God like?*—the God who has revealed himself as the Father of our Lord Jesus Christ—can be mostly encapsulated in three themes: he is loving, he is mighty, and he is holy.

## God is loving

In John 3:35 Jesus discloses one of the great secrets of the character of God. He tells Nicodemus that "the Father loves the Son, and has put everything in his hands." This short verse is one of the anchor points of Scripture, helping us orient all of Christian theology, because it tells us about the very foundation of God's will: he wants to be the Father. His will is to be the one that loves the Son.

It's incredible really, especially for us humans. You see, *my* existence, whatever it is that makes me *me*, has mostly been given to me from the outside. Being born as a person, in this time and among all these factors that have shaped me, is not something that I have chosen for myself but something that has been chosen for me. God's existence is different. No one ever willed to create him or influenced how he developed; no other force ever defined the parameters of how he could exist. God himself is, and has always been, totally in control of who he is. Whatever God is like, he is like that because that is just how he wants to be. John 3:35 is important, then, because it reveals how God has decided to shape his own existence. It teaches us that his eternal will is to be social, to be the Father who loves the Son and shares that love with the Spirit.

When the earliest Church discussed this theme, they called God the Father the *fountain* of the life of God, meaning that the whole being and essence of *who God is* springs from this fact of his Fatherhood. Because he chooses to be the loving Father, his 'one-ness' is a relational kind of one-ness that puts everything into the hands of the Son and the Spirit, showering upon them and sharing with them his love. The reason God is 'three Persons and one substance' is because he eternally wills to have an existence that is based on shared love—he has *decided* that the way he wants to live is to *be* the Father.

God's love, therefore, is not something that simply characterizes him like a deeply ingrained habit, it runs much deeper than that. Loving is not something that God *does*, it is *who he is*: "The Father loves the Son." The very existence of Father and Son, not just their relationship together, is rooted in the decision of God to love. This is why the climax of God's revelation to us comes in the person of the Son; every time Jesus calls God his 'Father' he is driving home the point that "God *is* love." (1J 4:16) Brunner calls this fundamental aspect of *who God is* his 'will-to-love', calling attention to the fact that being 'Father' is precisely the thing that God wants to be: God's will—the blueprint of his *being* and his actions—is grounded in a desire to be the archetype of love.

This is why when we try to describe God in words, we begin by saying that he is loving, because it reaches right to the core of who he is: he *is* the Father who loves the Son. And of course, because his very essence is 'loving-ness', when he acts, he acts in love. Thus we have encountered him, because thus he is. He creates in love, he cares for us in love, he saves in his love, he waits long and patiently for us because of his limitless will-to-love. Nietzsche says that at the root of humanity is a will-to-power, a desire to dominate in every relationship, bounded only by the limits of our strength. It's one of the reasons why his philosophy cannot understand God. God reaches out toward the Son—and toward creation—not with a desire to enslave and 'be the boss', but with a desire to love, to be the Father. Love never looks likes domination, even when it has the power to; love looks just like what we see Jesus to be. The more we come to know God, the less surprising we find this to be. For "the Father loves the Son, and has put everything into his hands," and it is this same God who "showed his great love for us by sending Christ to die for us while we were still sinners." (Ro 5:8) His life *is* love right to the very center and so it is only natural that his will-to-love overflows towards us with every step he takes into our lives to rescue us. What is God like? God is loving.

## God is mighty

To say that God is mighty is simply to say that God never lacks the strength he needs to accomplish his will-to-love.

Our natural definition of almightiness—the ability to do *anything*—is similar, but different in a significant way. If almightiness means *the ability to do anything*, then we are faced with the exhausting task of explaining whether God can do evil, or make a rock too big for God to move, and the like. *The ability to do anything* is a philosophical definition of almightiness, not a Christian—and certainly not a Biblical—one. It's a great way to talk about an army, or a battery, or a robot; it is a terrible way to talk about a Person. God the almighty is a divine Person, not a divine 'force' or 'it', and his almightiness is never just some sort of neutral or abstract reservoir of powerfulness that could be directed at *this* or *that* task, depending on the circumstances. The God of the Bible is never portrayed like that. With just his breath he overwhelms his enemies (Job 4:9, 2Th 2:8), but this doesn't mean he has some sort of 'super-breath' that no one can stand against, just waiting to spill out at every opportunity; he also speaks with Moses face to face and whispers to Elijah (Ex 33:11; 1K 19:12). God's almightiness isn't abstract, it is governed by—and for us, *defined* by—his will. And his will is to be the Father.

This is why God's actions are sometimes difficult for us to understand. The disciples, spending every day with Jesus for years, even right up to the crucifixion cannot seem to figure out why God's "mighty Savior from the royal line of his servant David" keeps talking about suffering and death rather than victory and thrones. (Lk 1:69) If he's the mighty one, why aren't we 'winning'? It was confusing for them because they—like we often do—were presuming the wrong kind of almightiness, the abstract kind. The goal of Christ's mission was never to 'win' in the way that the disciples understood winning, but to make peace between God and humanity. His goal was to love, and to make love possible. Nothing, not even our presuppositions about the way someone that mighty *ought* to act, could prevent him from accomplishing that goal. That's what it means to say he is the mighty one. As any parent who plays games with their kids knows, the goal is actually trying to figure out how to lose effectively (and surreptitiously), because the real point of the game is enjoying our relationship with the child. A father's might isn't measured by being so tough that he can't play Barbies, it's being so strong that he can. God's will is not a will-to-win, it's a will-to-love; at family game night, God always loses, even if we never quite figure out how, because that's just how mighty he is. He is free even to lower himself in the world's eyes if that's what it takes to make his will-to-love a reality. Nothing stands in the way of him being the Father.

Because of this, when we think through the group of qualities that are known as the 'attributes of God' (which is important), we must be very careful to only define them in light of the will of God to love, rather than as philosophical maximums. We should never (!) define God out of a dictionary, but only based on who he has revealed himself to be. That God is omnipotent, that there is nothing he wills that he cannot do, we have already seen. Closely related is his omnipresence, which means that he is always nearby, always present, in every context, and his omniscience, which means he knows and understands everything, including the past and the future. Isaiah communicates these themes together when he proclaims God's promise: "Do not be afraid, for I am with you. I will gather you and your children from east and west." (Is 43:5) God is omnipresent, he is with us; God is omniscient, he knows the future of us and of our children; God is omnipotent, nothing will stop him from putting his plan for us into action. And so we are not afraid. This is the personal God of Scripture: always mighty to save, always with us, always knowing what has happened and what's to come.

A further way of describing the might of God is by saying that he is *not* like us humans in all the ways that make us frail: he is immortal (not dying), infinite (not bound by time), and immutable (unchangeable). Here too we need to be careful. When we say, for example, that God does not change (Mal 3:6), that Jesus is always the same (Hb 13:8), this does not mean that God is inflexible or static. For God, immutability is *personal*, like the consistency or reliability of someone you know you can always depend on. Because he is consistent, we know we can trust him; because he is trustworthy, we know we can safely return his love. Jesus says: "Trust in God, and trust also in me;" (Jn 14:8) we are called to trust, even though we will never know everything about him. He is infinite after all. But we can trust him because we know that the same Jesus through whom the world was created— the same one who gave himself for our sins—is the one who already awaits us in the future, with a good plan for us; "Jesus is the same yesterday, today, and forever." We trust God because when he wanted to save us, he gave us his *real self*—not an emissary or a duplicate—so that we could see for ourselves what kind of God he really is. We trust him not because we know everything about him—his vastness is not limited by our understanding of it—but because he is consistent, because he does not change; the parts we know teach us to trust the parts we don't. All God's attributes, as with his almightiness, can only thus be understood in the context of his will to be the Father—he has the oneness he wants, the infinity he wants, the power he wants, the knowledge he wants, and the unchangeableness he wants—never is he burdened with traits that oppose him or get in his way.

The creeds call him *God the Father almighty* to remind us that he is never one without the other. He is never mighty with an almightiness that interrupts his being the Father; he is never the Father who would like to show his love but has a hard time figuring out how. He is the God who always finds a way to love without caging us in. He is the Father, he is the almighty. Always the two together. What is God like? God is mighty.

## God is holy

A third key aspect of God's character is his holiness; the unsoilable separateness and purity that he possesses in his nature and in all his actions. It is this element of his character that causes all of creation to tremble in fear before him, as the one who is *so* perfect, and so awesome that we are dust before him. But here too, we remember that God's holiness never impedes him from being who he is, the Father who loves the Son. His holiness is so great that all melt like wax before him, and yet, because his will is the will-to-love, he chooses to be holy in such a way that he makes his people holy, so that we can stand in—and enjoy—his presence. This balance is reflected in Isaiah 57:15 where God says through his prophet: "The high and lofty one who lives in eternity, the Holy One, says this: 'I live in the high and holy place with those whose spirits are contrite and humble. I restore the crushed spirit of the humble and revive the courage of those with repentant hearts.'" He is the holy and lofty one, too high and too great to approach, and yet at the same time the one who reaches down in love to restore the broken and revive the repentant, even though they fall short of his holiness.

God's holiness, then, means transcendence. He is above and 'set apart' both from this world and from anything unclean or impure, and cannot be grabbed at or reached up to. More than even that, it means that God is perfect in every regard, having no shortcomings and existing beyond even the possibility of accusation. Theologians sometimes describe this total perfection of God using the word *ineffable*, that is, that God is so perfect we have no words or ideas that are sufficient to say everything about him that ought to be said. (Mt 5:48) In his own being, not just considered in comparison to us, God is totally holy in a deeper and more real way than we can imagine.

God's holiness also includes his sinlessness: God does no wrong. (Dt 32:4) This theme is especially important when we come to the life of Jesus. Hebrews records that Jesus "faced all of the same testings we do, yet he did not sin." (4:15) Our God is holy with the kind of holiness that can climb down and live with us, even in the dirtiest spaces of our lives, without becoming ruined himself. God is totally separate from sin, but equally, he is so superabundant in purity that the things he comes in contact with—us!—are made clean by his touch. God is not holy like a new white shirt that you constantly fret about getting dirty; in the face of the griminess of sin, God's holiness overflows to make the impure, pure, and the dirty, clean. He is, as Leviticus 20:8 says, "the LORD who makes you holy." What is God like? God is holy.

*If I was preparing for accreditation I would . . .*
- Make sure I understood the meaning of the terms omnipresence, omniscience, and omnipotence, especially how they are defined in light of the will of God to love
- Be ready to explain why it is important that God is both Father and almighty
- Memorize Isaiah 57:15 and either John 3:35 or 1 John 4:16
- Read Emil Brunner's amazing sermon 'The Father Almighty' in *I Believe in the Living God*, chapter two

# 5. Creation

### *Why did God create?*

To be sure, God did not create because he *had* to, not in any sense of the word 'had to'. God's existence, unlike ours, is radically free; nothing ever forces his hand or exists alongside him in the shadows of eternity and coerces him into doing things. He was free to create, and it made him happy to do it, but he also would have been free not to. This means that he didn't create as a way of 'finding himself' or exploring and expressing himself in new ways so he could understand himself better and really complete his own existence (this is the basic idea that people are referring to when they talk about 'process theology'). Nor did he create because he had so much pent up 'cosmic energy' that he needed to find a project to help burn off some steam so that he would be able to relax in the evening. And he certainly didn't do it out of curiosity or to pass the time. God created *intentionally*; he doesn't do things on a whim. The only things God does are things he has planned to do, and his plan arises freely out of his will to be the loving Father, with no pressure at all from the outside (or the 'inside') leaning on him to do things in a way that's different from how he really wants them done. God created because he freely chose to create, not because he was compelled to do so. This is part of what it means when we say that God creates *ex nihilo*. *Ex nihilo* is a Latin phrase that literally means 'out of nothing', and includes the idea that God, unlike us, doesn't need any pre-existing materials when he decides to create something. It's what makes God's kind of creation so amazing: us humans can create paintings and buildings and scientific ideas, but only because God has already made colors and raw materials and the natural laws of the universe—and our own imaginations—available to us. Ultimately, we are able to create only because we ourselves have already been created. With God, creation means something different. When God creates, nothing sets the limits for him, he is totally free to do it however he likes, even in the absence of anything out of which to create. God creates without being constrained in any way. He didn't create because he had to.

Along the same lines, it is especially important to remember that God did not create because he was lonely. Remember that God, in his very essence, is sociable: he is Father, Son, and Spirit, living and sharing life together. He's not lonely. When we say that 'the Father loves the Son', it is more than just an abstract definition, it means that the Father and the Son and the Spirit are actually always hanging out together and having an awesome time of it: they love each other's company, and love spending their lives together. There is no neediness in the life of God that goes unsatisfied if he decides not to create, and it is misguided to think of creation as the act of a lonely (or bored!) God who is desperate to finally have some friends. God doesn't *need* more friends or some sort of cosmic 'spouse' to keep him company or entertain him. Of course he *wants* to be in relationship with us humans, and it makes him so very glad to call us his children, but he doesn't *need* us. Before he creates, God is already to-tally complete and happily content with who he is and the way he lives. God is never under pressure to create; God is never motivated by loneliness. God didn't create because he had to.

Why then did he create?

Well, I was pacing around our little living room last week (burning off some steam so that I would be able to relax in the evening), talking with my wife about my plans for the afternoon: "Well, I probably ought to get cracking on my next accreditation essay."

"Oh, which one do you have this week," she replied, lov-ingly feigning deep interest.

"Why did God create?"

At which point my daughter Flora, freshly home from kindergarten and dangling upside-down on the couch, cut into the conversation (as usual) and announced: "Because he *loves* us!"

And that's it really. God created because he loves us.

He created because he wanted to enjoy our company, and for us to enjoy his. He created out of a will-to-love. This is what Paul means in Ephesians 1:4-5 when he says that "even before he made the world, God loved us and . . . decided in advance to adopt us into his own family by bringing us to himself through Jesus Christ. This is what he wanted to do, and it gave him great pleasure."

You see, God's love is the kind of love that overflows. It is not a selfish love that only loves itself, or only loves when it gets paid back, but the kind of love that spills over and shares itself even when it isn't returned. My mom once told me that we pay back the love of our parents not primarily by loving them, but by loving their grand-kids the way that they loved us. God's love is that kind of love, just as happy seeing the effects of his love spill over to a loved third party as he would be receiving it back himself. Maybe more happy. The Father and Son never hog one another's love, they share their love—they share each other—with the Spirit. Father to Son to Spirit to Father: the love of God continually spills over from one Person to the others.

And in creation, this love of God overflows to us. God created because he had more than enough love to spare and so he wanted to share that love with us. God's motivation to create is like having extra tickets, and inviting your friends (especially the ones on home assignment from Indonesia) to come along, not because they need to come in order for you to get in, but because it feels great to share the joy of the game, both for you and for them. God sculpted this whole universe just because he knew how much pleasure we would get from exploring and using and living in it together.

God didn't create to fulfill an obligation, he created because he loves us. His whole plan is just this: to create us for love, with him and with one another, to share his love with us, and to make us able to respond with real love of our own. The Father wanted to see us have the fun of enjoying our everyday lives in the presence of the Son through the Spirit. He wanted us to have the experience of falling in love and living in love with one another. His chief purpose in creation was to create for himself an expansive family of persons enough like himself—made holy, able to love—that he could shower his kindness on forever. Romans says that this was

God's plan all along, that "his Son would be the firstborn among many brothers and sisters." (Ro 8:29) Of course, because of our sin it looked like we destroyed the plan, but even that could not stand in the way of God's power to achieve his will-to-love.

That's why God created, because God *is* love. He didn't have to create, he made all this only because he knew we'd love it, and made us because he wanted to share the overflow of his life with us. His will-to-create is grounded in his will-to-love. God created because he loves us.

### *If I was preparing for accreditation I would . . .*

- Make sure I understood the meaning of the term *ex nihilo*
- Memorize Ephesians 1:5 and Romans 8:29
- Rent *Lars and the Real Girl* starring Ryan Gosling with my mentor and talk about what it really means to love, and what that teaches us about why—and how—God created us (hint: the differences might be easier to spot than the similarities)

# 6. Humanity

*How do your Christian beliefs affect your understanding*
*of what it means to be human?*

Because I am a Christian I believe that human beings are precious to God on account of the fact that they have been specially created in his image. Humanity is, for me as a Christian, not merely the summit of some random evolutionary pyramid, but the result of the careful and intentional plan of God. What is more, I believe God's plan was to create us in his very own image: "God said, 'Let us make human beings in our image, to be like ourselves.' . . . So God created human beings in his own image. In the image of God he created them; male and female he created them." (Ge 1:26-27) However God created us, he did it intentionally, and he did it so that we, in some significant way, would be like himself.

But what does this mean, that we are created in the image God? Well, it doesn't mean our physical bodies are something that looks like his physical body because, as Jesus says, "God is spirit," (Jn 4:24) and simply doesn't have a physical body for us to look like. I also don't think that we have gone far enough if we just take the things that make us different from the other animals—say, rationality, creativity, and authority over the rest of creation—and say that these traits are the image of God in us. They are an important part of the image of God, but not the most fundamental one.

The most fundamental part of being created in God's image—in the likeness of the God who *is* love in his very being—is that we are creatures that can love: can receive the love of God and respond with real love of our own. Love is the way that we most resemble God, because God himself *is* love.

The image of God (sometimes referred to by its Latin translation *imago Dei*) cannot therefore be equated with our physical bodies, or limited by the collection of attributes that separate us from the animals, even if those traits are traits that God himself possesses in a higher or nobler degree. We don't learn about the image of God by looking at the animals, we learn about it by looking at God. Remember: the reason God created is because he loves us and because he wants to share his love with us. So he created us to be lovers, like himself. That is why humans are so special to God, not because we are the only animals that wear clothes, but because we are the only ones that have the capacity to love in the same sort of way that God loves, and to really understand and experience what it means to be loved by a heavenly Father.

Why, then, is it "not good for the man to be alone," as Genesis records? Why does God say, "I will make a helper who is just right for him"? (2:18) Surely not because Adam had too many chores in the garden of Eden. Rather, it was because he had been created to have a love that would overflow every day, just like God, first to Eve and then to the rest of his family. It was 'not good' for Adam to be alone because he was created in the image of God. He was created to love.

And *you* are created in God's image too. Bernard of Clairvaux, the twelfth century French monk, wrote that the highest level of love, higher even than loving God for God's own sake, was learning to love yourself, not out of selfishness, but because you yourself are someone that God loves. The highest love is loving yourself on account of the fact that God loves you. Because I am a Christian, I believe that people are extremely precious in the eyes of God—every one of us, even myself—because he created us in his own image, to love and to receive his love.

But also, because I am a Christian, I believe that this image is broken. Like an ancient statue with the face chipped off, there is a remnant and a suggestion of some features, but the original is well and truly gone. A smashed off face can no longer be reconstructed; it needs to be replaced. Because of our sin, everything is broken: the planet, us, our relationships, everything. But even so, this brokenness is not the end of the story, because in Jesus Christ the true image of God is once again seen in humanity. It is seen in Jesus, and it is seen the life of us Christians. Being a Christian does not merely mean being called by the name of Christ and merely having Jesus for an example, but actually having Christ himself dwell in us through his Spirit. "This means that anyone who belongs to Christ has become a new person. The old life is gone; a new life has begun!" (2Co 5:17)

Christ is our new face. Christ in us is our new humanity.

And so, because I am a Christian, and because I believe that humanity has been 're-faced' with God's image on account of Christ, I believe that God—and God's life—is the best pattern for me to understand who I am, and how I ought to live my life.

For example, understanding that I am created in the image

of God changes the way that I understand my marriage. God's love looks like this: The Father shares his life with a Son who is fully his own Person and who has a different role in the Godhead, if we can even use the word 'role' in reference to God. The Son is never the Sender, and the Father is never the Sent One (which is essentially the heresy of Patripassianism). The Father is called the head, and yet in every instance, Father and Son are always equal, and always one. All the more, the love of these two always overflows to include the Holy Spirit. This is the way that I have been created to love; this is the model for how I have been designed to function within my family. And so, whatever 'head' means, it never means 'boss' or 'master'; whatever 'role' means, it never means a difference in value; whatever 'one flesh' means, it never means that the identity of one is swallowed up in the other. Marriage in the image of God means loving by giving yourself away to the other, and letting your spouse be the person who *makes you who you are*; it means being willing to share one another—and the love and time that one another has—with other people and other things: children, single friends, family, favorite hobbies, work, ministry, play, even in-laws. Loving in a marriage means learning to love in a way that overflows, rather than in a selfish or self-promoting way. I don't know everything about what it takes to be a family like God planned it, far from it, but I know for certain that I am a better dad and assuredly a better husband when I remember to think about my place in the family as somebody who has been created to love like God loves. Being created in God's image makes—should make—our Christian marriages different.

I think it makes everything different. I care about the planet because people have to live on it, and I care about them and their situation. Although it is sometimes difficult, I begin to learn how to see others as God's special creation, and to love them for his sake. I don't hog my love, sharing it only with the people I enjoy the most and who really love me back: I try to find ways to become the kind of person whose love overflows. I enjoy and explore the world God put me in, receiving it as the gift of a Father who wants to give good things to his children.

When it comes to my humanity, being a Christian changes everything: it is a new understanding, a new life, and a new pattern and ability for living. It is all these things because Christ has come to live within me by his Holy Spirit, and has remade the broken image of God in my life, giving me the ability to truly love and to receive the love of my heavenly Father. Christ, you see, has become my new face. And so both the way I look at the world and the way the world sees me have begun to reflect the fact that I am a special treasure in the sight of God, someone who bears his very own image.

### *If I was preparing for accreditation I would . . .*
- Make sure that I could explain what it means that humanity is created in the image of God
- Be aware of the term *imago Dei*
- Memorize Genesis 1:27 and 2 Corinthians 5:17

# 7. Sin

## *Describe the problem of Sin*

In the beginning, sin was not a problem. God's creation was good, as he had created it to be, and all its parts functioned well together. God did not create sin. What he did do, however, was create human beings with the real ability to reject the plan that he had put into place. You see, although more complex definitions are possible, it is probably most helpful to think of sin as basically the decision to choose a plan that is not God's plan. "Remember, it is a sin to know what you ought to do and then not do it," (Jas 4:17) which is what our first parents did in the Garden of Eden when they decided to follow the serpent's instructions rather than God's. But why was that even possible? Why were Adam and Eve so easily able to find their way out of God's plan?

The sinning was certainly not God's plan, but the ability to do so was. What I mean is this. Genesis says that "the LORD God made all sorts of trees grow up from the ground—trees that were beautiful and that produced delicious fruit." It sounds great, doesn't it. But as we read on we find that "in the middle of the garden he placed the tree of life and the tree of the knowledge of good and evil." (Ge 2:9) Both these trees? In the middle? Wasn't one of them the tree that if they ate from they would surely die? Why was it in the middle of the garden instead of at the edge?

For of course it makes sense that God would place the tree of *life* in the middle of the garden. God never makes it difficult to find him or to choose his plan. And his whole purpose in creation was that Adam and Eve—and us—would enjoy *life* with him and with one another forever. In the garden, God's plan—*life*—was always easy to find. But God also planted this other tree, the tree of the knowledge of good and evil, right beside the tree of life, right where we would continually come across it. And he did this for the same reason he created: because he loves us.

If God's plan was the only plan we had to choose from, then at the end of the day we would really be little more than slaves, or hamsters, or robots that responded to him because we didn't have the capacity for anything else. But God's will was never to create robots; you don't share your love with a robot, or with a prisoner. God's love is *real* love, the kind that never tries to force its recipient to love back, and so, even though he is the Lord of the universe, he made it easy for Adam and Eve to walk away from him and choose to go their own way. He gave them the real freedom to make their own plan if they wanted to. If he hadn't, we humans would have never been able to answer his love with the free response of our own hearts and genuinely love him back. If he hadn't, we'd be robots. That's the reason why there was the possibility for two kinds of plans in the garden: God's plan, and the plan where you choose your own plan.

So, in the beginning, sin was not a problem. And yet when Adam and Eve sinned, when they decided that they would choose a different plan for themselves that was not God's plan, sin became a problem for all of humanity, and for all of creation. Just as parents make decisions every day that shape and determine their children's future—where to live, who to play with, whether to start piano lessons or soccer, what to eat—the decision that Adam and Eve made has had a determining effect on all of their descendants, including us. And just as some parental decisions are irreversible upon their children—say, emigration or nutrition—the decision that the parents of all humanity made to choose 'not God's plan' has had an irreversible effect on everything else since. Because of their sin, we humans have all become separated from God, totally lacking the ability to return things to the way they once were. In the Church, we call this event 'the fall' to catch precisely this meaning: that something final and disastrous happened at that moment which cannot now be undone or overcome.

When Adam and Eve ate the forbidden fruit, they made the decision on behalf of all creation to choose the plan that was not God's plan. Just as they had been given the authority to name the animals, they were given the real freedom to set their own direction, which has now become our direction. In choosing to reject God's plan—in choosing to sin—Adam and Eve placed the whole of creation under the dominion of Sin. (This is the root meaning of the phrase 'original sin', that we have inherited a world both broken and dominated by Sin; the denial of this theme, claiming that human free will is strong enough on its own to enable some people to live free from sin, is, in its essence, the heresy of 'Pelagianism'.) We are sinners from the start; each of us. Augustine reminds us that babies aren't any more sinless than anyone else—even if they look it—they just usually lack the ability to force their self-will on those around them like the rest of us do. As humans, we cannot keep from starting to sin, and once we have started, we cannot stop. Jesus puts it this way: "I tell you the truth, everyone who sins is a slave of sin." (Jn 8:34)

Because, then, we now live in a world ruled by Sin, everything is broken, and our world has really become a messed up place. Under the control of Sin, we have become not only the enemies of God, but enemies of one another, because each of 'our own plans' tends to get in the way of everyone else's until we can only really succeed by crushing one another, and often our own selves, even if that wasn't how we intended our plan to turn out. Sin means hostility toward God and harm to one another because it means choosing to do things not the way God planned them to be done.

This is the problem of Sin. It dominates our lives and guides our world according to a plan that is not God's plan, a plan that we cannot stop continuing to choose. It's why our relationships continually break down, and why we find friendship with God to be impossible; it is why the earth itself is corrupted, and why we cannot even really love or understand our own selves satisfactorily. When Paul says that "the wages of sin is death," (Ro 6:23) he means that eternal and spiritual death awaits the one who lives under the dominion of Sin, but also that every sin creates and anticipates death in and around the life of the sinner, even if the effects are sometimes difficult to see. The problem of Sin means that we live in death every day—spiritual death, physical death, social death, personal death, environmental death—and that we continually reinforce death ourselves even though we hate it. It means that every one of us, aside from the grace of God, has been set from birth on a path that leads without exception to what Revelation calls the 'second death'. It means we can do nothing to escape the decisive and irreparable hostility that exists between us and God and the unending competition and contention that characterizes all our relationships. God's plan for the garden was *life*; the problem of Sin is death.

And it is a problem from which no one is exempt. All of us are born into this same broken world and have inherited the same broken sinful nature. Sin affects everyone, and its only remedy is found in Jesus Christ. Especially in the Alliance, we use the word 'lostness' to talk about how this brokenness of Sin affects every person on the planet. The Bible states it explicitly: "everyone has sinned; we all fall short of God's glorious standard." (Ro 3:23) As much as we might sometimes like to imagine the opposite to be the case, there simply aren't people who through their natural piety or religious intensity have broken out on their own from under the power of Sin and escaped death. It is an impossibility. Doing it 'on your own' is very the definition of Sin; it's the exact thing Adam and Eve did to give the world over to the command of Sin in the first place. 'On your own' is the thing preeminently *un*able to free us from our slavery to Sin, our destructive compulsion to do it on our own even when we don't want to. Every person is lost apart from Jesus Christ.

Jesus, however, not only defeated Sin itself on the cross, but as the 'second Adam' has reinstated for us the possibility of choosing God's plan through his own obedience to it. Jesus breaks the power of Sin expressly by being willing to not do it 'on his own', but by choosing to submit to the plan of God the Father. It is his life in us that can finally liberate us from Sin and make us free from sinning: free at last to truly see God's plan and free at last to choose it. "There is salvation in no one else! God has given no other name under heaven by which we must be saved." (Ac 4:12)

The creation was good, and God's plan was good, but we used our freedom to choose our own plan, to choose separation from God. In doing so our freedom was taken from us and our lives became defined by Sin and by sinning; ever since, Sin has meant death for us both in this life and the life to come. Death. That's the problem of Sin. But it is a problem that has a solution, Jesus Christ, the one who reconciled us to God, recreated us in God's own image, and restored God's good plan—the plan of *life*.

### *If I was preparing for accreditation I would . . .*

- Be aware that sometimes theological books use the word 'Sin' (spelled with a capital 'S') to talk about the cosmic presence and results of Sin in the world, and 'sin' (spelled with a lower-case 's') to talk about the sinful actions of individuals
- Be ready to discuss (and succinctly define) the terms 'fall' and 'lostness'
- Memorize Romans 3:23, Romans 6:23, and probably John 8:34

# 8. Jesus Christ

*What are the important elements of a Christian response to the question: 'Who is Jesus Christ?'*

## Jesus Christ is fully human, just like we are

In the fall after my freshman year at college I took a job as a framing carpenter and have been building things out of wood, on and off, ever since. It's been especially tough on my fingers. I have stapled them, hammered them, pinched them, crushed them, frozen them, electrocuted them, put thousands of splinters in them, and, once, driven a three inch spike into them with the air nailer. And so this is my problem: I know that Jesus worked for years as a carpenter too, just like me, but my inclination is to say that maybe Jesus is too perfect to have ever hit his fingers.

But you know what? He isn't. Jesus was the kind of carpenter who mashed his pinky every now and then, because that's precisely what it means to be a real human carpenter. It's not sin, it's just being a real human with a real job and living in our real world, a world that is totally broken by Sin. And so he knows the pinch and burn that comes when you clip the back edge of your ring finger with a hammer, along with all the other far more serious things, because he actually was a normal human being just like you and me. Jesus does not merely share a few traits in common with us; he is "in every respect like us, his brothers and sisters," (Hb 2:17) having a human body like ours, a human nature like ours, a human personality like ours, human emotions like ours, and having endured all the limitations that come with being a regular human.

This is what Paul is getting at when he says in Galatians 4:4 that "God sent his Son, born of a woman, subject to the law." Jesus came into this world just like we do, as a baby, and was subject to all the same kinds of restrictions and conditions that we are. Jesus did not come as a 'super-man'—armed with a collection of powers that insulated him from the real world—but as an *actual* man, a human being just like us. He hit his fingers in the wood shop, annoyed his parents, got frustrated with his disciples, cried his eyes out when one of his best friends died, and lived as a subject to the law of this world his whole life long. This is the marvel of the incarnation, isn't it, that Jesus, the eternal Son of God, became an actual human being, just like us.

Why? He did it because it was necessary for our salvation. You see, just as our whole human nature was broken by the fall, our whole human nature needed to be restored and recreated by God. To do that, God the Son brought the whole of our broken human nature into himself and purified all of it by making it his own. As Gregory of Nazianzus (one of my favorite theologians) said, "that which He has not assumed He has not healed; but that which is united to His Godhead is also saved." The thing is this, Jesus only rescues the humanity he carries with him to the cross. If Jesus only took up a part of what makes me a real human being, then only a part of me has truly been saved. In fact, part of what it means to call Christ our healer is acknowledging that he has indeed taken real human flesh and real human nature into his own Person and restored it by his touch. Being human was essential to his mission. Hebrews 2:14 says that "because God's children are human beings—made of flesh and blood—the Son also became flesh and blood. For only as a human being could he die, and only by dying could he break the power of the devil, who had the power of death." Jesus Christ is our savior because he was willing to become everything that we are.

The humanity of Jesus is therefore serious business. 1 John 4:2-3 says that anyone who denies "that Jesus came in a real body . . . has the spirit of the Antichrist," (the technical term for denying the full humanity of Jesus like this is 'Docetism'). If Jesus Christ was not fully human, then he never truly gave himself on the cross for our sins, and our humanity has never truly been redeemed. But he *was* fully human, human just like you and me, and he *did* give himself up to rescue us from our sins and create a new way of being human. The first critical thing to remember about Jesus Christ is that he became a totally real human being, just like we are.

### Jesus Christ is fully God, just like the Father is

In the Old Testament we are introduced to God as the one who calls the universe into being and who sets the standard for life and morality, the one who judges the nations and chooses one of them to be his very own and bring his salvation to all people. He is the great and only God who rules over all creation, both seen and unseen. In Exodus 3:14-15 he gives Moses his name, so that his people can know him and call upon him. This name—usually written 'LORD' in our Bibles—is 'Yahweh' (sometimes given as 'Jehovah' in older writing). It is Yahweh who placed Adam and Eve in the Garden, Yahweh who invited Abraham to be his friend, Yahweh who rescued his people from Egypt, Yahweh who cast down the walls of Jericho, Yahweh who selected David as king, and Yahweh who spoke through the prophets.

Only with this picture of God before us—of all those stories we know about our mighty God at work in the Old Testament, of Israel singing together at the defeat of Pharaoh at the Red Sea: "The LORD is a warrior; Yahweh is his name!" (Ex 15:3)—can we really give a Christian answer to the question 'Who is Jesus Christ?'. Because, as George Pardington rightly says, Jesus Christ is the Yahweh of the Old Testament. This doesn't mean that the Son is the Father, definitely not. What it means is that the name Yahweh, the personal Hebrew name for God in the Old Testament, applies just as equally to the Son as it does to the Father.

And so who is Jesus Christ? He is LORD, he is totally God, just like the Father is. Jesus Christ is Yahweh. It is Christ who spoke to Moses from the burning bush, Christ who met Joshua with sword in hand outside Jericho, Christ who sat with Abraham outside Sodom, and Christ who wrestled with Jacob and negotiated with Gideon.

The Church of the New Testament, of course, calls him 'Lord' hundreds of times, using the same word their own Bibles used for Yahweh. (Most of the New Testament writers, along with the majority of the earliest Church, used the Greek translation of the Old Testament, called the 'Septuagint'; the New Testament word 'Lord' is the same Greek word that the Septuagint used to translate 'Yahweh' in the Old Testament;

the significance of applying this term to Jesus would therefore have been unmistakably clear for both them and their early readers.) More explicit yet, there are several passages where the New Testament writers quote a passage of the Old Testament about Yahweh and tell us expressly that this passage applies to Jesus. Thus we learn the true depth of belief in the earliest Church, and what the first Christians meant when they confessed, right from the very start, that "Jesus Christ is Lord."

The Gospels are all thus unafraid to use name Yahweh to refer to Jesus. Quoting Isaiah 40:3 they present John the Baptist as the one preaching repentance in anticipation of the arrival of Jesus the Messiah and calling out, "Prepare the way for the LORD's coming." (Mt 3:3, Mk 1:3, Lk 3:4, Jn 1:23) Prepare the way for the LORD, clear the road for Yahweh; Kavin Rowe calls this "an indisputable citation from the Old Testament," and writes that, in Luke and Acts, "to speak of Yahweh is to speak of Jesus and vice versa." Hebrews too points to Jesus as Yahweh, quoting 1:10-12 from Psalm 102, as does Peter, quoting 1 Peter 3:12-15 from Psalm 34.

And in perhaps the clearest passage of all, the apostle Paul shows us what 'Lord' means for him when he talks about the identity of our Lord Jesus Christ. Inspired by the Holy Spirit, Paul writes in Romans 10:9 that "if you confess with your mouth that Jesus is Lord and believe in your heart that God raised him from the dead, you will be saved." And then to make sure we all understand what he means by saying 'confess Jesus as Lord', he reiterates the passage he is quoting from the Old Testament, Joel 2:32, where it says that "everyone who calls on the name of the LORD will be saved." (Ro 10:13) Everyone who calls on the name of Yahweh will be saved; everyone who confesses Jesus as LORD will be saved.

Jesus is the LORD—is Yahweh—just as the Father is, even if this Trinitarian mystery is difficult for us to fully comprehend. It's why Jesus can say that "the Father and I are one" in John 10:30, why he doesn't rebuke Thomas who falls down at his feet worshiping him as "my Lord and my God", why John calls him "the only true God," why both Paul and Peter call him "our God and savior," and why "the Jewish leaders tried all the harder to find a way to kill him. For he not only broke the Sabbath, he called God his Father, thereby making himself equal with God." (Jn 20:28; 1J 5:20; Ti 2:13; 2P 1:1; Jn 5:18). Being 'God' is not an abstract quality that Jesus possesses in equal measure with the Father and the Spirit; God—Yahweh—is *who he is*, and we cannot rightly talk about Jesus if we fail to remember this. Jesus is not merely *similar* to the Father; he is the same God, the same Yahweh, that the Father is. Sometimes, to make this point clear, theologians say that Jesus is 'of one substance with the Father' (the Greek term is *homoousios*) as a way of expressing as carefully as possible that the Son is God in all and every way that the Father is, and not just the same *kind* of being as the Father (the latter being the heresy of Arianism). In human history, the clearest marker of Jesus' divine nature is his resurrection—"he was shown to be the Son of God when he was raised from the dead by the power of the Holy Spirit." (Ro 1:4)—but his divinity did not begin there. "In the beginning," says the Scripture, "the Word already existed. The Word was with God, and the Word was God." (Jn 1:1) It is this Word, this pre-existent and fully divine Son of God, who became a human so that he could save us. The second critical thing to remember about Jesus Christ is that he is fully God—fully Yahweh—just like the Father is.

## The humanity and deity of Jesus Christ are united in his one Person

There are two bad options for describing the way that the human and divine natures of Jesus Christ are united together. The first bad option is thinking that his two natures are somehow melded or combined together to form really just one nature (which is, broadly speaking, the heresy of Monophysitism). This could mean that they are mixed together to form a new kind of nature that is partly human and partly divine, or that Jesus' divine nature functions as his soul/mind/will while his human nature serves to provide him with a body. The problem with this option is that it leaves Christ without a full human nature (which would mean that some parts of *our* humanity are not redeemed) or without a full divine nature (so that he is not Yahweh with the authority to forgive sins and create us anew). At its worst, this kind of thinking can end up producing a Jesus Christ who is neither human nor divine, but some sort of 'third kind of thing'. It is never the right decision to describe Christ by saying that his two natures are somehow combined into one.

The other bad option for talking about the human and divine natures of Jesus is to consider them so separately from one another that it becomes impossible to think of Jesus any longer as one real person (which is, roughly, the heresy of Nestorianism). Christianity doesn't teach two Christs or two Jesuses, one human and the other divine: Jesus Christ is one real Person. When we describe his two natures, we cannot let ourselves stop short of talking about how in Jesus Christ they are genuinely united together: that was the whole point of the incarnation, wasn't it? There is only one Son; we should never allow our eagerness to preserve the completeness of his two natures to in the end cause ourselves to break his Person into two.

So, we cannot merge the natures, and we cannot undermine the unity of his Person. What then do we do? The short version of the answer (and the one you should memorize) is that we always remember that Jesus possesses two full natures, one human and one divine, that have been miraculously united in his one Person: two natures, one Person. Put another way, in the incarnation the eternal Son of God took on another nature—a human nature—and incorporated it into his own being without diminishing or distorting the divine nature he already had, and without subdividing his Person into parts.

The joining together of the human and the divine in Jesus Christ is a union that takes place *in his Person*; his own Person is both the 'location' of the union and the source of the power that unifies his two natures. Paul paints a picture of this in 2 Corinthians 4:6 when he says that "God, who said, 'Let there be light in the darkness,' has made this light shine in our hearts so we could know the glory of God that is seen in the face of Jesus Christ." When we look at the face of Christ we see both the man Jesus and the glory of the eternal God the Son. One face—one real Person—two natures. The (important) technical word that is used to describe this relationship is 'hypostatic union'. Remember: *hypostasis* is just the Greek word for Person. The 'hypostatic union' is not a style of uniting or a name for the product of the two natures.

Rather, it is primarily a statement describing *the location of the union*: Christ's two natures are united in his Person—his *hypostasis*—without being mixed together or breaking his Person into parts. When I look into the face of my savior I see both the man Jesus and the ever-living Yahweh: two natures, one Person.

Who is Jesus Christ? Fully human, just as much a human as I am; fully God, just as much God as the Father is. These two natures aren't blurred together, nor do they stretch him so that he begins to break apart. Rather, in his own almighty Person, he holds the two together without difficulty and without sacrificing the one for the other. Like Paul said: "Christ himself was an Israelite as far as his human nature is concerned. And he is God, the one who rules over everything and is worthy of eternal praise! Amen." (Ro 9:5)

### *If I was preparing for accreditation I would . . .*

- Read the first two chapters of Harry Blamires' incredible book on this topic, *The Offering of Man*
- Make sure I understood the term 'hypostatic union', and the definition 'two natures, one Person (hypostasis)'
- Memorize Romans 9:5, Galatians 4:4, and John 1:1
- Be aware of the important phrase 'of one substance with the Father'

# 9. Christ our Savior

*What is the significance of Jesus' death and resurrection?*

### Jesus has set us free from our sins

As any Christian can tell you—even the newest or youngest one—the reason Jesus died on the cross was to take away our sins. Isn't that great! Because of Christ you are forgiven. You really are. The ultimate significance of Jesus' death and resurrection is that he has somehow made peace between us and God by the shedding of his blood. His act of obedient sacrifice has cleansed us of our sins and put an end to the state of hostility that existed between us and God; because of the cross, God counts our faith in Jesus as real righteousness. This is what Paul means when he says that "God made Christ, who never sinned, to be the offering for our sin, so that we could be made right with God through Christ." (2Co 5:21)

In theological language, this act of Christ on the cross to make peace between humanity and God—to "set us free from the penalty of sins we had committed" and "bring us home safely to God" by the shedding of his blood—is called the atonement. (Hb 9:15, 1P 3:18) Remember, the problem of Sin is death: death in this life all around us and eternal death in the life to come. When the Son of God became a man, he took this problem upon himself and made himself subject to death, just as we are. But because he never sinned, never chose to 'do it on his own' but to always submit to the Father's plan, he death was a different kind of death than ours. For us, death is the ultimate and understandable consequence of a life filled with sinning. When Jesus Christ died on the cross, however, it was as "a sacrifice that would take away the sins of the people," not as the enactment of a punishment that he himself deserved. (Hb 2:17)

Why did he do it? Why did he "offer himself as a sacrifice for us"? (Eph 5:2) He did it because he loves us. God, knowing that we were helpless on our own, but filled with love for us and deeply caring that our friendship with him should be restored, took it upon himself to do all of the work to make things right between us, to reconcile us to himself, even "while we were still sinners." (Ro 5:8) It is the greatest theme of the Christian faith, that "God loved the world so much that he gave his one and only Son, so that everyone who believes in him will not perish but have eternal life." (Jn 3:16) The significance of the death and resurrection of Jesus is not merely the cosmic defeat of Sin by our mighty God so as to make the salvation of humanity possible, but, for the believer, a very personal demonstration of the love of God for me. Christ died not just for the sins of the world, but for me, and for my family, to atone for *our* sins and to bring *us* safely home to God.

## Jesus truly is both son of man and Son of God

This very genuine and specific love of God for you and me, the kind of love that motivated his willingness to intervene in our situation even at great personal cost, is a reflection of his character. You see, the death and resurrection of Jesus

Christ—*what he did* for us—is always the result of *who he is* as the God of love who became human for our sake. The atonement is therefore a crucial demonstration of his identity. In his death we are reminded that the Son of God genuinely became 100% human, just like us. The story of his life was of course not identical to the story of each of ours, that's not what it means to be a human being. As Thomas Oden reminds us in his book *The Word of Life*, being human means being particular: having one place of birth, one gender, one set of experiences, one life's journey, and one experience of death. Jesus was not like us because he was exactly the same as you or me or anyone else, but because he was a unique person just like each one of us is. Because of his death we are assured of the completeness of his humanity, that the incarnation really goes all the way down, right to the bottom of what it means to be human, and that Jesus really did take the totality of human experience upon himself. Not every possible experience, but the actual experience of a genuine human life, like ours, the kind that occurs in one place and at one time, and goes from a beginning to an end. But more than even that, his burial teaches us that we have nothing to fear from what comes after death (and before our own resurrection at the end of time) because, wherever it is that we go in the moment after death, our 'elder brother' Jesus has gone there ahead of us and emerged as Lord and victor over it.

So too, just as the death of Christ is the clearest marker of his full humanity, his resurrection means that without doubt he truly is the Son of God. As the apostle Paul says in Romans 1:4, "he was shown to be the Son of God when he was raised from the dead by the power of the Holy Spirit."

His resurrection to a glorified and perfected body—the kind of body we ourselves will one day possess—is the ultimate vindication of everything that he taught about who he is and why he had come. Because he was raised again we know that he really is 'God with us', really is *one* with the Father, and really is the Good Shepherd come to seek and save the lost. The resurrection means that God really "was in Christ, reconciling the world to himself, no longer counting people's sins against them." (2Co 5:19) And so, when Paul sums up the Good News of Christianity in 2 Timothy 2:8, he simply challenges the reader to "always remember that Jesus Christ, a descendant of King David, was raised from the dead. This is the Good News I preach." Jesus is the descendant of David, and he died: he truly is a human. And he has been raised from the dead: he truly is the divine Son of God he claimed to be. For Paul, this was enough to encapsulate the whole heart of the gospel: the true God of love became a true human, and died and rose again, so that he could save us. The death and resurrection of Jesus—the climax of his mission to save us—is also the most important testimony to his identity as both the son of man and the Son of God.

## Jesus is the victor over Sin and Death

Finally, his death and resurrection mean that Jesus has decisively triumphed over the power of Sin and Death in the world. It's part of the reason he came: "to destroy the works of the devil." (1J 3:8) Jesus is the victor over Sin, having put himself under the influence of our Sin dominated world his whole life long and yet never caving to its dominion. And he is the victor over Death, having died, but yet conquering the grave and returning to a full and glorified life. Jesus says of himself in Revelation 1:18, "I am the living one. I died, but look—I am alive forever and ever! And I hold the keys of death and the grave."

To say that Jesus has risen, then, means more than just saying that Jesus himself is alive, it means that the whole range of domination that Sin previously held over our lives has been taken away. In part, this means that the power which Sin had exerted over us, so that we could do nothing but keep on sinning, was broken at the cross. Because of Christ's victory over Sin, we do not have to live according to that old pattern any more. Jesus Christ, our new Adam, has made a new way of being human, a way that does not have to live as a slave to sin. This is why in the Alliance we say that 'sanctification is in the atonement': at the cross, Jesus not only atoned for our sins, but also totally dismantled Sin's control over us and made it possible for us to live lives that are pleasing to God.

Our healing too is 'in the atonement', not meaning something altogether too mystical or magical, but rather the simple truth that God still heals people in response to the prayers of his people, and that when he does so, his healing power is based in the authority that Jesus, because of his cosmic victory over Death, has over sickness and death in our present world. The power of Sin and Satan was to keep us as sinners and to direct all of our existence toward frailty and death; the power of the atonement—the power of Christ Jesus, the victor over Sin—is to set us free from the necessity of sinning and to give us the opportunity to place our health and our lives in the hands of the one who loves us, rather than into the fist of our enemy. Because Christ has died and risen—because the heritage of Sin's control over humanity has been defeated—we are once again free to entrust ourselves to God's plan rather than go it on our own. The cross and the empty tomb mean that Christ's victory over Sin, Death, and the Devil is complete.

### *If I was preparing for accreditation I would . . .*

- Read "The Grand Miracle" by C. S. Lewis, from his book *God in the Dock*, chapter nine
- Make sure I understood the term 'atonement' and could explain it to a person in my church
- Memorize 2 Corinthians 5:21 and either 1 Peter 3:18 or Hebrews 9:28

# 10. Salvation

*Describe the process of salvation*

**"Even before he made the world, God loved us" (Eph 1:4)**

The first thing that happened in the process of your and my salvation was that God loved. God loved long before he created, with the kind of love that included making a plan to come and rescue us if we needed it, even if that meant his own suffering. Maybe there is a sense that true love always looks like this, that it is always accompanied by this kind of willingness to suffer for the good of one's beloved; when we consider the love of God, it is certainly the case. God knew what he was doing when he created, he knew that our salvation would be necessary, but his decision to create anyway means that the delight of sharing his life with us was worth more to him than the cost he knew he would have to pay to save us. God saves us for the same reason he creates: because he loves us. The process of salvation begins long before the moment of salvation; the story of our salvation begins with love.

Because God loves us—has always loved us—he cares about what happens to us. And so, because on our own we are totally lost, God reaches out to us himself. He calls out to us by various means, puts significant people into our lives, protects us, places himself in our path, opens our eyes so that we can see him, gives us life's blessings, and keeps working in our hearts in all sorts of ways we cannot see, even when we ourselves are unaware of his activity. Most importantly, it is God himself who gives us the ability (and the courage) to turn away from our sins and to call out to him in faith.

All of this—all the ways that God reaches out to us even though our hearts are cold toward him—is wrapped up in the meaning of the word 'grace': the blessing and favor that God puts in our lives even though we don't deserve it. In particular, the kind of grace that comes before the moment of our salvation is sometimes called 'prevenient grace' (prevenient means 'coming before'), and it looks different in each of our lives. Some of us were born into Christian families where we heard the story about God's love for us since . . . well, probably since before we could really even understand it. Some others of us have longer journeys that have led to God, or less direct ones. The important thing is not that we all take exactly the same road to faith, but that we learn to recognize that exactly the same God has been at work in the lives of each of us, on whichever road we have been on. Long before we ever considered him, he was calling us, guiding us, and making it possible for us to come home safely to him. You see, on our own we truly are lost; not one of us is able to find his or her own way or achieve his or her own salvation. It's not just that we lack the power to fix our broken relationship with God; on our own we don't want to. Truth be told, we don't even really conceive of God or consider his friendship a possibility. But God, because he loves us, begins working in our lives while we are still a long way off. The process of our salvation doesn't begin with our repentance; we can't even manage that in our own strength. Salvation begins with a grace that comes long before that, a grace that woos us and waits for us, and that makes repentance and faith possible for our otherwise cold and dead hearts. It is God who makes our reconciliation with himself possible, and who wants it—and works for it—long before we ever do. The story of salvation begins with love.

## "Believe in the Lord Jesus and you will be saved" (Ac 16:31)

Following the long working of God's love in our hearts, in the life of every Christian there comes one critical moment where we respond to God's call and he graciously welcomes us in to his family. This decisive point in time—conversion, the moment of our salvation—has two essential halves, both empowered by God's grace. The first half is our repentance and belief. We call it 'ours' not because we manage to achieve it all on our own; 'our' repentance and faith is something we can exercise only because God in his kindness gives us the strength to do so. But because God loves us—with a real love, a love that never forces—he never saves us against our own will. He calls us and waits for us; he woos us and puts himself in our path; he goes so far as to reach into our sinful and cold hearts and make them alive enough to respond to his call and aware enough to want to. In one sense, it is all God's doing. But at the same time it is we who do the actual repenting and the actual returning to him. This is why Peter declares to his listeners on the day of Pentecost: "Each of you must repent of your sins, turn to God, and be baptized." (Ac 2:38) God does the saving, God does the convicting, God even does the making us able to turn, but somehow he also makes room for us to be a part of the story of our own salvation. *We* must repent; *we* must turn to God and be baptized. God doesn't save us against our will, even in the midst of being the one who makes us able to repent and believe. Following God's love, the process of salvation continues with our repentance and our faith.

The second essential half of the moment of salvation is God's response to our repentance and faith. At our conversion, four things come to us from the hand of God, not one after another, but all together as a piece, and all because of Jesus Christ: we are forgiven, we are justified, we are born again, and we are given the Holy Spirit. These four themes can be found together in 2 Corinthians 5, one of the great 'salvation' chapters of the Bible. In verse 19 we hear the good news that, in Christ, God no longer counts our sins against us: we are forgiven. In verse 21 Paul reminds us that we have been "made right with God through Christ": we have been justified. God has fixed what was broken in the relationship between us and him, and counts us as righteous because of Christ. He counts us as his friends. Verse 17 says that "anyone who belongs to Christ has become a new person. The old life is gone; a new life has begun!" What a great hope! God's great salvation means I don't have to live according to all those same patterns I used to live by, because I am not that person anymore; I have been born again as a citizen of the kingdom of God. (The technical term for this is 'regeneration'.) In verse 5 we are reminded that as believers we are now never alone because "God himself . . . has given us his Spirit."

Of course, because God works in each of our hearts in a unique and individual way, the *experience* of conversion is a little different for each of us, even if the underlying pattern of God's work in us remains the same. What I mean is this. When Kari (who is now my wife) and I started dating, I was not in love. I was 'crushed' to be sure, but, truth be told, my feelings were probably closer simply to the delight of just hanging around with someone as pretty and interesting as she was (and still is!). Little by little, though, I did fall in love. I can't exactly say when. I remember the moment when it struck me that I wanted to ask her to marry me, the moment she said 'yes', and many other moments along the way, but the moment of falling in love I can only really narrow down to a season of a few months in 1998 and '99 when my heart went from 'like' to something much more.

In some ways, I think that the experience of salvation is a little like the moment of falling in love. Many Christians—and many who are in love—can decisively point to one day, or one hour when they knew for the first time. Others cannot. For them, it is a 'longer moment', like mine, that cannot be narrowed down or remembered so specifically, but is nevertheless just as real. Billy Graham, in one of the best and most straightforward books on salvation I have read, wrote about this reality saying that "becoming a Christian can be a crisis experience in your life, or it can be a process with a climactic moment of which you may or may not be conscious." In the life of every Christian there *is* a moment of salvation, even if we do not remember or recognize precisely when it was. This is of course especially relevant for those believers who have grown up in the Church and maybe cannot even remember a time when they were outside of God's family. In the life of a healthy and growing Christian, however, being unaware of the precise moment of our salvation doesn't mean we are unsaved anymore than being unaware of the moment I fell in love with my wife means that she remains unloved. Salvation is a process, but it is a process that always reaches a central, climactic moment—that critical point where God brings us from death to life. It's a moment that happens uniquely in the experience of every Christian whether they remember it or not.

But what really happens in this moment? Some Christian people say that the experience of salvation is like entering into a 'personal relationship' with God. In a lot of ways, that's what it *is* like. But, as wonderful as this phrase is, we need to be careful how we use it, especially about stretching it's meaning too far. Having a personal relationship with God doesn't mean that Jesus takes you bowling or goes with you to the waterpark. That's why he gave us the Church, so that we could really be flesh and blood friends to each other, the kind we all need, and would love and care for one another. Normal friendships are part of God's plan, not something that gets replaced by becoming a Christian. Rather, the word 'personal', when we use it to talk about our relationship with God, is simply a way of saying that each of us are saved individually, by a divine *Person*—not by some sort of impersonal 'force' or 'cosmic happening'—and that the result of our salvation is that God genuinely comes to know us, and care about us, in the kind of way our other friends do, and that we begin to get to know him too. 'Personal relationship' doesn't mean that we stop having friends and start having God, but just this: although God himself is totally unique and unlike anything else we know, God's way of relating to us in salvation looks more like the normal way that friends relate to friends than maybe it does to anything else that we have the ability to describe. In many ways, even though it has its limitations, 'personal relationship' is perhaps one of the best words we have to describe salvation, as long as we are careful not to overextend it.

**"God, who began the good work within you, will continue his work until it is finally finished on the day when Christ Jesus returns." (Php 1:6)**

Just as salvation does not begin out of the blue at the moment of our conversion, it does not end there either. Now to be sure, as far as the work of Christ on the cross is concerned, salvation is finished. Christ suffered once, and not one thing needs to be added to his death and resurrection—to his great victory over Sin and Death—to make it sufficient to break us free from the power of Sin and bring us home safely to God. In fact, nothing *can* be added to it. But at the same time, from our perspective as the ones being saved, salvation is not complete. Salvation is not a 'one time' work that God completes in us in an afternoon, but a long process whereby God reaches out to us, rescues us, and then patiently works in us to make us fit for an eternal life of enjoying one another's company. This part of the story of salvation, where "the Lord—who is the Spirit—makes us more and more like him as we are changed into his glorious image," is what is meant by the term sanctification, or perfection. (2Co 3:18) God has brought me safely home, but now he is making me perfect, just like his Son Jesus. The story of our salvation extends beyond that beautiful instant of our conversion in both directions. God's grace works ahead of conversion making us ready, and continues to work after it by making us holy.

And one day the process of our salvation will be finished when Christ comes again and God, by his grace, makes us glorious.

You see, our salvation is something that has happened already—we genuinely have been saved—but if we really read our New Testament carefully, we see again and again how our salvation is presented as something in the future, something that we are still waiting for (two good examples are Ro 5:9 and 1P 1:5). And this matches our experience, doesn't it. We know that we have been saved, and as we look around it is easy to see how God has changed our situation, but we also see the ways that God has allowed our situation to remain the same, even when our situation is a bad one. And it's not always to build our character, or to teach us a valuable lesson; sometimes it's just because we live in a world that has been broken to pieces by Sin.

If we think about salvation as something that is already finished, it can be tempting to presume that we ought not to have these kind of deeply distressing experiences in our lives like non-Christians do. And in one sense, our salvation *is* finished: Christ's victory over Sin and Death is totally complete and doesn't need to have *anything* added to it. But in another really important sense, our salvation is hardly complete at all, but only really just beginning. You see, the story of salvation includes not just this life, but also our life to come, our glorification when Christ comes again as king. When we compare our lives right now to our hopes of heaven it is perhaps easier to see how much saving work God has decided to wait on before completing, both in and around us. For although God, in his kindness, places foretastes of the kind of experiences we are going to have then into our lives right now, a lot of times—maybe most of the time—God allows Christian people to live through really difficult situations. Not because they haven't prayed enough or aren't holy enough, but simply on account of the fact that our salvation is something that is very much still to come. 2 Corinthians 12 reminds us that this was certainly Paul's experience; it has been so for very many others as well.

Pastorally, this means it is usually particularly insensitive to talk to Christian people about the long term problems in their life as if they had never had the idea to pray about them, or have never tried praying with real faith. And of course we ought always to pray for these kind of long term problems, the kind that people have been living with for years, but as pastors we also need to take seriously the fact that the process of our salvation has not yet been brought to a close and that, until it is, there will always be suffering and difficult situations in the Church. Of course, sometimes God will reach in and change a situation that has up until now caused intense suffering—God still does the miraculous!— and sometimes people need to be challenged to pray with greater faith. We ought never forget the instruction of Jesus in Luke 18:1 to "always pray and never give up." If you are a pastor: pray. Pray for the people God has put under your care. But remember too that our salvation won't ever be finished this side of our glorification. We live in a world that, in spite of Christ's death on the cross, is still dominated by Sin. There is a lot of horrible suffering in our lives and the lives of people all around us, and there will always be a lot of horrible junk that true Christian people in our churches have to deal with. Some of it—lots of it—God will not take away before Jesus comes again: our salvation is something that is still coming, something still in the future. And so sometimes the place God has for you and me will be suffering alongside a Christian brother or sister in the midst of a situation that God will not make right until Jesus comes again, when he will truly wipe away every tear, even though from where we sit right now we can't imagine how.

"And all of this is a gift from God." (2Co 5:18) All of salvation, not just what God does for us in that one climactic conversion moment in response to our repentance and faith, but all that he does all along the way, before and after, reaching out to us, causing us to hear his voice, convicting us of our sin, enabling our faith and our repentance, making us right with him and restoring our position in the family even though we don't deserve it, creating us anew, and finally perfecting and completing his work in us. All of it, the whole process of salvation, is a gift from God. And he gives it happily because he loves us.

### *If I was preparing for accreditation I would . . .*

- Read chapters 9-13 of Billy Graham's book *Peace with God*
- Memorize Romans 10:9 and 1 John 1:9
- Learn the terms justification, regeneration, and prevenient grace
- Be ready to discuss the process of salvation in my own life

# 11. Christ our Healer

*How is physical healing related to*
*the person and work of Jesus?*

When we try to understand and explain the place of physical healing in the church today—especially as pastors—we need to be careful to remember that we are no longer living in the 1890's. In the 1890's the Alliance faced questions about the *limits* of divine healing, like whether or not Christians should take medicine or go to the doctor when they are sick, or whether or not to vaccinate their children. But no one is asking those kinds of questions today. Not because the healing power of God has changed, or his availability to heal in the name of Jesus Christ, but because just about everything else has, and that makes talking about healing a little complex for us. In particular, it means we have to learn to be flexible enough to offer answers to the questions that people really have, not the ones they used to have, even if that makes us feel a little distant from our predecessors and the kind of language they used to formulate our understanding of healing.

So. Is divine healing still a real possibility for me? It is. It genuinely is. But that's the question people in our churches are really asking these days, if we are honest enough to state it so bluntly. In that context, how can we best understand healing in a way that makes sense to the modern Christian?

You see, in spite of our changing world, and especially

the incredible advance of medical science in the last century or so, God still heals. There are three important reasons why we should still teach—and prayerfully expect—divine healing as a normal part of the Christian life: because God cares about our bodies, because Jesus has defeated death on the cross, and because the Bible teaches healing in a way that is comprehensible even to a modern person.

## God cares about our bodies

The first reason why healing is a possibility for the church today is that God's attitude towards our bodies remains unchanged. For God, our bodies are not the part of us he tolerates for the time being so long as they don't get in the way of the bit is really interested in: the soul. God didn't create us as souls, he created us as humans, as beings who have souls *and* bodies, and he cares just as much about the physical me as he does about the spiritual me.

Think back to the garden of Eden. Adam and Eve sinned and God was about to banish them from the garden forever. But before he did so, "the LORD God made clothing from animal skins for Adam and his wife." (Ge 3:21) Why would he do that? Why make clothes? He did it because he knew that fig leaves wouldn't cut it in the face of cold and heat and work and danger and everything else they were about to encounter. He did it to take care of their bodies. Remember: the first sign that God hasn't given up on us and still has a plan to save us isn't a sacrificial system or a covenant, it's clothes. Right from the start, God was ready to show that he cared about our bodies.

Or think back to the ministry of Jesus and the apostles.

On the one hand, the message of the kingdom is surely a 'heart' ministry. The gospel is a call to repent and believe. But on the other hand it is just as equally a 'body' ministry. The two go together. What are the marks of the kingdom? In Jesus words: "the blind see, the lame walk, the lepers are cured, the deaf hear, the dead are raised to life, and the Good News is being preached to the poor." (Lk 7:22) Healing *and* preaching; the restoration of our bodies *and* our souls. The same Jesus Christ who took up and inhabited our real human flesh—and redeemed it at the cross—healed and fed and paid attention to physical people his whole ministry long. It was a part of the declaration of his coming kingdom: God still cares about your body.

And think forward to the resurrection. God's plan isn't for us to stop having bodies altogether, but to receive bodies that have been transformed and perfected. At the end of the age God will transform us into people who possess the kind of humanity that we see in Jesus himself after his resurrection: powerful and perfected to be sure, but recognizable people who walk, and eat, and touch, and talk. As Paul says, "we will put on heavenly bodies; we will not be spirits without bodies." (2Co 5:3) To God, the body is not something extra that eventually gets done away with, but an important and permanent part of who we are. God's plan for us is a plan that includes us having bodies. Forever.

Sickness, you see, is not a problem with how God has made our bodies, or a reflection of the value he places on them. Sickness is not a body problem, it's a Sin problem.

Sickness is a part of this world because death is; it's the foretaste of death that we battle as long as we are alive. And death itself, of course, is a part of our world because it is the partner and consequence of Sin. Sin, sickness, death: all of it together is the work of the devil, even on the days when he convinces us that it is just a part of the natural order of things. It is not. We suffer from sickness and brace ourselves for death because the devil has from the first convinced us to give ourselves over to living our lives our own way instead of God's way. We are trapped in our sicknesses because we are trapped in our sins. Sickness is not usually the consequence of some specific sin, although it sometimes is, but rather the consequence of living in a world that is governed by Sin—by 'not God's plan'—as a guiding principle. We, collectively, are sick because we, collectively, are sinners. The experience of sickness is physical or psychological, but the foundation of sickness is Sin itself.

It wasn't God's plan for us to get sick and then to die; God's plan was life. And so, his decision to rescue us from the dominion of Sin includes our bodies just as much as our souls. Matthew, quoting Isaiah, describes Jesus as the one who "took our sicknesses and removed our diseases." (Mt 8:17) Of course, just like the other parts of his plan, we have to wait until the end of the age to see its full completion—the complete restoration of all our bodies will not occur until Jesus comes again—but we still get to see glimpses of that plan breaking in even now. That's what healing is, it's God's impatience at waiting to give us all the benefits of living in his glorious kingdom. And so he reveals a bit here, and a bit there. Sometimes seemingly all in a bunch and sometimes more spread out. God heals us because he cares about our bodies; one day he will make them perfect.

God cares: it's why he has commanded every Christian to be involved in taking care of the physical needs of the weak and the poor. God knows that their physical sorrow is real sorrow, and has given the Church to the poor so that he can make their suffering less. The Church's mission is to act in the world like Christ acted—to really *be* the body of Christ—and that means consistent ministry to the physical needs of our neighbors. God cares about the problem of sickness just as much as we do. Healing is a real possibility for the church today because God cares about our bodies.

## Jesus has defeated death

One of the great gifts that God has given humankind is medicine. Not only do our bodies have an incredible resiliency to heal themselves and recover from sickness and injury (like in the story of Epaphroditus in Philippians 2:25-27), but God has scattered throughout his creation all kinds of plants and herbs and minerals that can be refined and employed to alleviate pain and overcome the impact of sickness in society. Yet as marvelous as medicine is, we all know, don't we, that its effects are ultimately temporary. We can be made well by antibiotics or surgical transplants, but we fall ill again, and all of us eventually die. This doesn't mean that healthcare is bad or wrong; quite the opposite. It is God's plan that we would use medicine—meaning both the skillful knowledge of doctors and the drugs that we develop from the world around us—to fight back against sickness, he just never intended, say, penicillin to be considered the limit of his ability to deliver victory over sickness and death to us. Medical care is good, truly good, and comes to us directly from the hand of God—it is he who made us to be creative and attentive, who gave us a desire to investigate and solve the problems that face us, and who surrounded us with a world full of medicinal resources to explore—but it is not enough.

Fundamentally, sickness is a supernatural problem, and so it needs more of a solution than natural medicine can ever give. It needs a supernatural solution. As A. B. Simpson said, because "sickness has come into the world through sin . . . it must be got out of the world through God's great remedy for sin, the cross of Jesus Christ." And that is what has happened.

Healing is a possibility for the Church today because Jesus has defeated Sin and death on the cross. Jesus is God's supernatural solution to the problem of sickness.

This doesn't of course mean that everybody gets healed, or that sickness is never a problem for a Christian person living in faith. That doesn't match either our own experience or the testimony of Scripture. What it does mean is that God has the power to heal right now, because the source of sickness—Sin and death—has already been crushed by Jesus Christ. This is what we mean in the Alliance when we say that 'healing is in the atonement'. Power for healing in the Church today originates not from our own faith or from using just the right words when we pray; it comes to us from the cross and the empty tomb of Jesus Christ because that is the place where sickness and death met their ruin.

Although the victory of Christ is already complete, we don't yet see its full effect, and we won't until Jesus comes again as king. When that happens, Sin and death will be wiped out for ever: Paul says that "the last enemy to be destroyed is death." (1Co 15:26) Because God has been willing to wait for you and me, and for all the others who will come and participate in it, the full expression of his kingdom has not yet arrived, even though the decisive battle has already taken place. Sin is still in the world, and because of Sin, death. But, at the same time, the resurrection has already begun: Christ has been raised. And us Christians? We live sort of caught in between, already in the kingdom, but not yet seeing its final manifestation. The power to perfectly glorify our bodies already rests in Jesus' hands, but he waits to express that power so that his whole family can be brought safely home first.

When healing happens in our churches—and it does still happen—it happens because Jesus has already stripped death of its authority over us. Healing is like a foreshadowing of the coming kingdom. Then, when Christ's kingdom finally arrives in full, our bodies will be made perfect. In the mean time, because Christ himself has already risen from the grave as the victor over death, he is able and available to reach into our lives and give us a partial taste of the life that we will all experience together in heaven. We continue to teach healing as one of the normal things that happen in the Church today because we believe that Christ the Victor lives among us.

## The Bible's teaching on healing is comprehensible

The Bible—and Church history—is full of all sorts of marvelous stories about God's power to heal. Like when Peter healed Aeneas, "who had been paralyzed and bedridden for eight years. Peter said to him, 'Aeneas, Jesus Christ heals you! Get up, and roll up your sleeping mat!' And he was healed instantly." (Ac 9:33-34) And God still heals this way, in an instant.

Our experience, however, often feels much more mundane. We have prayed a lot of times, but met few people with a story like Aeneas. Which is why we do ourselves a disservice if the 'Aeneas stories' are the only ones we ever tell in the Church, because instantaneous healing is not the only way that God responds to sickness and to prayer for healing in the Bible. Nor is it the only way that our fathers and mothers in the Alliance experienced it: George Pardington's incredible story is, for example, a testimony to God's *gradual* healing. We don't have to pretend that our experience is something that it is not in order to talk about the idea that God is still able to heal. We need to believe that God can still do the miraculous, but we don't have to be intellectually dishonest with ourselves. Divine healing can still be taught to modern people because the story of healing in the Bible is actually not so far distant from our own modern experience.

Sometimes, instead of healing us instantaneously, God promises us healing, but the healing itself comes more slowly. This was the experience of Hezekiah. Fearing for his life in the face of sickness, he cried and prayed, and God sent him a message through Isaiah saying, "I will heal you . . . three days from now." (2Ki 20:5) Hezekiah was healed, but he was not healed in an instant. Sometimes God works in our bodies this way. He gives us a peace that we will recover, even if it takes some time.

Sometimes God tells us 'no' when we ask for healing, but gives us his peace. In 2 Corinthians God tells Paul that although he has prayed, God will not heal him, and instead gives him the promise: "My grace is all you need. My power works best in weakness." (2Co 12:9) This matches the experience of many Christians today too. God has said that he will not heal, but offers the comfort of his grace to strengthen the believer who has sought him for healing.

Sometimes God tells us nothing, responding to our prayers for healing with silence, like he did when David prayed for the healing of his son. Reflecting back, David talks about how he didn't know what God was going to do. He says, "I fasted and wept while the child was alive, for I said, 'Perhaps the LORD will be gracious to me and let the child live.'" (2Sa 12:22) The child died. There are times when we pray for healing for ourselves or others and God answers with silence.

Sometimes God answers us, but his answer is not what we want to hear. This happened to Ahaziah, king of Israel, after he was badly injured in an accident at home. God sent him a message through Elijah the prophet saying, "you will never leave the bed you are lying on; you will surely die." (2K 1:16)

And sometimes, don't miss this one, God responds to us by telling us to take the right kind of medicine to deal with our problem. God's message to Timothy through Paul on account of the fact that he was "sick so often," was not to pray more, or to fast, but to realize that God had already provided for his healing by a natural means: "Don't drink only water. You ought to drink a little wine for the sake of your stomach." (1Ti 5:23) For Paul, inspired by the Holy Spirit, going through a normal medical treatment wasn't a mark of lack of faith, it was the mark of prudent intelligence. Remember, all the 'natural' tools for healthy living that we find around us—diet, exercise, water, medicine, driving safely, taking a day off once a week so that stress doesn't build up—are ultimately '*super*natural'. It is God himself who has filled this world with all these things so that we can use them to help our bodies flourish. Having faith means choosing a healthy lifestyle; being a Christian means taking care of your body.

At times, I feel that if I want to be a person who believes in divine healing I have to believe in it in only the first kind of way, the instantaneous way, but that is not correct. All of these are ways that God has responded in the past when people have prayed to him and asked for healing, and they represent some of the ways that he still responds. So keep asking! Keep believing! Always pray, and never give up. But as a pastor, or a friend, be sensitive too. Healing doesn't always happen in an instant, and even if it never does, that doesn't mean that God is not at work, or that he never heals. Don't give up on your belief in God's ability to restore our broken bodies, but don't compartmentalize it either. Divine healing is still comprehensible, even in the light of our own very modern—and, often, very mundane feeling—experience. God is still available to answer when we seek him for divine healing, just not always in the way we expect it.

### God still heals

So, if God always can, why does he not simply always heal? The most honest answer we can probably give is 'I don't know'. Maybe lack of faith, maybe. Maybe lack of asking. Certainly never the lack of using the right formula when we pray. That is magic, not Christianity. God cannot be, and does not need to be, forced by us to heal. God can heal you, or your situation—giving his healing touch to your mind or to your body—even if you have not seen his healing yet. And even if God does not heal us, it does not mean that he cannot, or that he does not any longer, or that we are too unholy or unsanctified to receive it. To be sure, if God has pointed out sin in our lives but we are unwilling to let it go, that will stand in the way of our being healed: sin and sickness go hand in hand. But God doesn't heal as some kind of reward for good behavior. Remember, the apostle Paul himself was horribly sick when he first preached to the Galatians. Healing doesn't come as the result of meticulously following some magic formula or by being a good enough Christian, it comes at God's good pleasure and on account of the death and resurrection of his Son Jesus. Healing involves praying, it involves asking, and it involves rejecting Sin and submitting ourselves to God's plan, but the ultimate ground of healing is never your or my own personal holiness or even the quantity of our faith. The ground of our healing is the work of Jesus Christ on the cross. Healing is something we ought to consider to be a normal part of Christian experience—and ought to expect and to teach in our churches—because Christ has already won the victory. God still heals; God is still ready to share the great victory of Christ with us as a reminder of the promise of our life to come.

### If I was preparing for accreditation I would . . .

- Make sure I understood the meaning of the phrase 'healing in the atonement'
- Memorize 1 Peter 2:24 and James 5:17
- Exercise

# 12. The Holy Spirit

*What are the important elements of a Christian response to the question: 'Who is the Holy Spirit?'*

The Holy Spirit is probably harder for us to visualize than either the Father or the Son: ought we to think of him as a bird, or maybe a ghost-like spirit, as a wind or a force, or perhaps something else altogether? Are we even allowed to? How *should* we describe him? Historically, the place of the Holy Spirit within the Trinity and in the life of the Church has been less controversial than that of the Son, and so there are comparatively fewer written materials from the first centuries of the Church about him that we can look back to and draw upon. This doesn't mean that the Church was unsure about him; in fact, it means the opposite. Regarding the Son, there was all manner of debate over his exact relation to the Father and exactly what it meant to call him Lord. But there has almost always been such a broad consensus within the Church regarding the Holy Spirit that the Fathers mostly found it sufficient simply to acknowledge him in prayer and in the sacraments (as described in the important book *On the Holy Spirit* by Basil the Great) and confess him as "the Lord and giver of life, who proceeds from the Father and the Son, and who with the Father and the Son is worshiped and glorified" like we find in the *Nicene Creed*. And so in one sense, just to say that is probably enough to answer the question

"Who is the Holy Spirit?" But if we push just a little farther, three important themes emerge that can help to clarify our thoughts and provide constructive boundaries to all our discussions about the Holy Spirit: he is a divine Person, he is fully God just like the Father and the Son, and he is the one who brings the personal and life-giving presence of God into our lives.

### The Holy Spirit is personal

For all eternity, before there ever was an earth or a universe, God the Holy Spirit was enjoying the loving companionship of God the Father and God the Son. He loved both the Father and the Son perfectly, in such a way that his love for the one always overflowed to include the other. There has never been a time when the Spirit had not yet begun to express himself happily in relationship with Father and Son, and there never will be a time when he stops. The Holy Spirit is an eternal participant in God's life of love; the Spirit is a divine Person, just like the Father and the Son.

Because he is a Person, it is always wrong to talk about the Spirit using abstract or impersonal language, as if he were only a 'force' like gravity that affects us all even though we cannot see it. Of course, in the same way that we use words like 'fortress' or 'lion' to talk about the Father and the Son, we can use metaphorical language when we describe the Holy Spirit, especially biblical ideas like 'wind' or 'fire'. But we must always be careful to never allow ourselves to use these kinds of descriptions to depersonalize him, no more than we would ever allow our description of God as our fortress to mean that he never moves and cannot speak or feel. We especially cannot refer to the Holy Spirit with the word 'it'. To call the Holy Spirit 'it' wouldn't just be offensive, it would be nonsensical, like if I called one of my brothers or some other person that I know 'it', as in: 'I am so happy for my brother because it is getting married in a few months'. Talking like that is bizarre. 'It' is a word for things, not for persons, and the Holy Spirit is in fact far more deeply and truly personal than even you and I are. We are the ones who are created in his image, never vice versa. The Spirit is a Person—not a force, not an 'it'. He is a divine Person, just like the Father and the Son.

When we talk about the Holy Spirit, then, we use the word 'he' instead, not because the Spirit is male, but because he is *personal*, and, until recently, the word 'he' was universally understood as the best non-gender-specific personal pronoun available in English. Other languages, such as Indonesian, do not have this problem because they treat pronouns and gender in different ways. But irrespective of one's grammar, the principle is the same: the Holy Spirit is never a male or a man, but also not ever a female or the element of the Trinity that expresses 'womanhood' as a counterbalance to Father and Son. He is especially not some bizarre combination of the two. The Holy Spirit does not have a gender; he is *above* being male or female. *Both* genders were created in his image. No, the Holy Spirit is not a male, but he is nevertheless a 'he' in English, in the now increasingly archaic, gender neutral sense of the word. We call the Holy Spirit 'he' not because he is gendered or male, but because he is personal.

Because he is personal, it is no surprise for us to find that the Bible talks about him in personal kinds of ways. Jesus himself tells his disciples that the Spirit who is coming will be "another Advocate," another one like himself, and teaches that the Spirit will be sent from the Father, just as he himself was, as a divine Person bearing the fullness of the Godhead into the midst of our lives. (Jn 14:16) Elsewhere, the Scriptures state that the Spirit experiences personal emotions like sorrow (Eph 4:30) and can be lied to (Ac 5:3), just like the other persons we know. But most important of all, the Bible presents the Holy Spirit alongside the Father and the Son in verses like Matthew 28:19 and John 4:24 as an equal, a Person who is loved by them and shares their love. We understand the Spirit as personal not because he has had the title of 'personhood' forced upon him, but because he actually functions as a loving and healthy Person. The very being of God is his loving; the Holy Spirit is a Person.

### The Holy Spirit is fully God, just like the Son and the Father

In the same way that the Holy Spirit is fully personal, so too is he fully divine, just like God the Father and God the Son. He is God the Holy Spirit: worthy of our prayers, worthy of our adoration, and worthy of all the same worship we offer to Father and Son. It is into his name that we are baptized. He is equal to the Father and the Son in authority, in divinity, in time, in power, in knowledge, in glory, and in love. He is the one true God. With the Father and the Son, he shared God's Triune decision to create and was happy to participate. And so in the pages of the Bible we first meet the Spirit in Genesis 1:2. He is no late addition or a creation brought into being for the benefit of the Church, although he is eager to come and be with us, to care for us, and to have us enjoy his presence. The Holy Spirit loves us. He *is* love. His love, the love shared between him and the Father and the Son, is what makes up the very essence of God's being. Just like Father and Son, he has no need of us, but he delights in letting his perfect love flow over into our lives, and he calls to us and empowers us so that we might freely respond with love of our own.

The Holy Spirit is fully God, just like the Father and Son. He is fully eternal, fully glorious, fully unlimited and un-fathomable, and fully powerful. Most of all, he is fully love.

## The Holy Spirit brings the presence of God into our lives

Finally, the Holy Spirit is the one who makes the presence of God real in our lives, by coming and living in and among us in the Church, and by bringing with him all the life and the blessing that the presence of God represents. It is the Holy Spirit who reaches out towards us even before we reach out to him, and softens our hearts with grace so that we can respond to him. It is the Spirit who convicts us of our sinful-ness and challenges us—and enables us—to repent. It is the Holy Spirit who stood behind the prophets and the writers of Scripture, guiding them and helping them, so that the things that they said and wrote would be for us the very words of God. And it is God the Spirit who shines the light of his presence on the pages of Scripture so that the reader who is genuinely seeking God himself and his leading in his or her life can really find it there. It is the Spirit who brings the presence of the risen Christ into our presence in the sacra-ments, who joins us and leads us in worship, and the Spirit who fills and accompanies us Christians so that we know

God's presence in the midst of every experience, whether good or bad.

And of course, because he has filled us—or, put another way, because we have been baptized with his presence—we have received incredible gifts and spiritual power. The Holy Spirit is a real Person, baptism in the Spirit is a real experience, and living life in a totally different way is a real possibility for you and for me. On my own I know I cannot forgive, even if I want to. I cannot stop getting mad, or stop hating and coveting, or start loving even the people I care about the most in that true kind of selfless way that God does. On my own, all I can manage is to just keep on living like this. But that's not how life looks with the Spirit. Sometimes, I know, I decide to block him out or not let him work freely. But it doesn't ever have to be like that: being filled with the Spirit—being sanctified—means that the Spirit can change any part of me, that he is even able to change and repair *all* the broken bits. In fact, because God the Holy Spirit is present in my life, it means that those things *are* changing. And as I see the way that the Spirit is forming me into the image of Jesus Christ, God the Son, I am given great courage and assurance, because as the Spirit changes me I begin to see that I really am a child of God, that I really have been saved by faith in Jesus Christ, and that I really will enjoy his company forever in heaven. This is what Paul means when he says that "the Spirit is God's guarantee that he will give us the inheritance he promised and that he has purchased us to be his own people." (Eph 1:14) The presence of the Spirit, the way that he makes me able to love like God loves, and the practical assurance of my salvation are all connected.

The Bible also describes more than a dozen ways that God gives special gifts to Christian people; probably the gifts that are listed in the New Testament are not even all the ways that God the Holy Spirit can specially and supernaturally work through one or another of us in the Church. And the Holy Spirit *still* gives the Church a wide variety of gifts for ministry today, depending on the needs of the local body: helping, teaching, giving, preaching, speaking in different languages, interpreting, working miracles, having supernatural insight, and many others. Because it is the same Holy Spirit who is at work within and among us, he is still capable of working in all these ways, and still does. But because our lives and the needs of our churches are different in many large and small ways from how things were two thousand years ago, we should not expect our experience to always be exactly like the kind we read about in the New Testament. It ought to have strong similarities, but it will probably never be identical. And so we need to guard against a desire for certain gifts over others in order to try to be more like the early Church, and most of all against prioritizing the experience of the gifts themselves over the Giver who brings them into our life: the Holy Spirit. Spiritual gifts are not items or objects to collect; they are the expression of the Spirit himself working through the Christian. We never *have* a certain gift; what we *have* is the life of God the Holy Spirit in us and working through us in miraculous ways, to help build up the body through things like administration, or showing mercy, or healing. The goal—indeed the mark—of the deeper Christian life is a growing closeness with the Spirit, not the supernatural power that comes when he is present. The gift *is* the

Giver. The Holy Spirit is the one who brings God's life-giving presence right into the middle of my life and the life of my local church; the Holy Spirit is the personal God of the universe at work in us and among us.

***If I was preparing for accreditation I would . . .***
- Memorize John 14:16-17 and 2 Corinthians 3:17
- Read Isaac Keita's essay "Person and Work of the Holy Spirit," especially the last couple pages
- Be aware that the Alliance position on speaking in tongues is 'expectation without agenda', which means that while we do not emphasize tongue-speaking as a necessary part of the life of every sanctified Christian (as in Pentecostalism), we do not in any way deny it as a normal and acceptable expression of the Holy Spirit within the life of the believer, even in public worship, but in that case there has to be an interpreter
- Read the excellent, short essay "Spiritual Gifts: Expectation without Agenda" online at the Alliance website, cmalliance.org.

# 13. Christ our Sanctifier

## What does it mean to be sanctified?

To really understand sanctification we need to gather together three related ideas: that sanctification is something accomplished by Christ, that it is something brought into effect by the Holy Spirit, and that it is something that can be seen in the way I live my life from day to day.

First, understanding sanctification means understanding where it comes from. Sanctification is a possibility for us only because Christ's great victory over Sin is already accomplished; our holiness is grounded in his work on the cross. As Jesus said, "I give myself as a holy sacrifice for them so that they can be made holy." (Jn 17:19) At Calvary, Jesus not only paid the penalty for our sins, but in fact defeated Sin itself. Romans 6:10 says that "when he died, he died once *to break the power of sin*." That's what we really needed. We know, don't we, that we cannot break the power of sin in our own lives. We cannot stop doing life 'on our own', even when we recognize that doing it on our own always ends up in disaster one way or another. We cannot, but Christ can. He can step in and set us free from Sin in our own lives because for him, Sin is already a defeated enemy. For the Christian, being sanctified means sharing in this victory that Christ has already won, it means that the power of Sin is being broken in my life not by me, but by Jesus Christ.

The atonement is the story of Christ's victory over Sin in the world; sanctification is the story of Christ's victory over Sin in me. He is able to accomplish it in me because the ultimate victory—his cosmic defeat of Sin, death and the Devil—has already been won by means of the cross. This is why Romans says that "when we died with Christ we were set free from the power of sin." (6:7) Sanctification is something that is for us—it's a changed life—but it something *for us* only inasmuch as it is something *because of him*. In the Alliance, we talk about this idea by saying that 'sanctification is *in the atonement*'. It's a way of expressing our belief that you simply cannot understand what sanctification is unless you see it in the light of the death and resurrection of Jesus Christ. The possibility of our sanctification comes from the certainty of the atonement; the way I live my life today can look different because of that victory that Jesus won on the cross back then.

Second, sanctification is something that the Holy Spirit does inside of me. "This is the secret," writes Paul, "Christ lives in you." (Col 1:27) Being sanctified means that the Holy Spirit brings the victory of Christ into our lives by personally coming in and taking up residence within us. 1 Corinthians 3:16 presents it as the plainest truth of the Christian life: "Don't you realize that all of you together are the temple of God and that the Spirit of God lives in you?" Of course there is never a time when the believer is *without* the Spirit, but yet sanctification describes a life filled with the Holy Spirit in a way that is richer and fuller. This is what Jesus was teaching his disciples about the Holy Spirit in John 14:17: "you know him, because he lives with you now and later will be in you." For the disciples, just like for us, there are two kinds of knowing the presence of the Spirit, *with* and *in*. The Holy Spirit is *with* every Christian from the moment of conversion, but there is a deeper kind of God's presence in our lives that happens when we give ourselves over completely to him (the older word for this is 'consecration') and God responds by filling us with his Spirit. Being sanctified means, somehow, having God *in* us through the Holy Spirit. From the perspective of our own Christian experience, this coming *in*—this filling or baptizing which actually brings the presence of Christ and his victory over Sin *into* our lives—is maybe the most important thing the Holy Spirit does for us. Sanctification is therefore not primarily a change in *what I do*, but a change in *who I am*, which then impacts how I live. I become a temple. It is not something I do—or try harder at—it is not even that God patches over or mends some part of me to make me look better on the outside. Sanctification is a supernatural recreating of me from the inside out as the dwelling place of God. What does it mean to be sanctified? "This is the secret: Christ lives in you."

Finally, although sanctification is something that happens inside of me, it's a change that can be seen in the way I live. It's a little like a healthy marriage. Even though you cannot see the marriage, you see the way that the love between husband and wife spills over and effects every other part of life. And so no one assesses the strength of a marriage by asking what the wedding ceremony was like; we look at the way that the marriage partners give themselves in love one for another right now. You can't get to a marriage without a wedding, but at the same time, once you get there, the way that you live together as a married couple will continue to take on more and more significance than the day when it all started. So too the sanctified life. It is genuinely something that *has happened*, and that history is important, but sanctification is so much the more something that *is happening*. The sanctified *living*—the Christ life—is in the long run far more important than the sanctification event itself. And just like married life, even though you cannot see the sanctification, you can often see how this new way of being reaches into all the other corners of our day to day life—and changes how we act there—even when you cannot exactly explain how. Sanctification is something that happens inside of me—it's a change in who I am—but the difference can be seen in the way that I live.

## Holy living and effective service

This last aspect of sanctification, this part that you can often see—maybe not always in others, but for sure in yourself—has two parts: holy living and effective service. 'Holy living' is perhaps both the most 'common sense' aspect of the Christian doctrine of sanctification as well as the biggest stumbling block to understanding it. Being sanctified genuinely means living differently, because God has implanted in me the desire to do right—to "live a life filled with love" (Eph 5:2)—and provided me with the power to actually choose to do it. It doesn't however mean that I become immune to making mistakes or falling short. Rather, sanctification means that I am becoming the perfect specimen of right where I am at and that I am learning to obediently do just what God is asking of me right now. (Ps 19:12-13)

Because Christ lives in me through the Holy Spirit, it has become possible for me to live a holy life. Of course I cannot myself become God; and, thankfully, God doesn't hold me to that standard. What I can do, moment by moment, is overcome temptations that I know are wrong—it is God who gives me the ability to do that—and choose to live my life God's way. (1Co 10:13) Because God himself lives within me, every part of me is being changed into the likeness of the Son, and that's a change you can see. (1Th 5:23) The first practical outworking of the sanctified life is holiness.

Sanctification also means gaining the ability to truly serve God effectively. It's a little astonishing, but at the beginning of the book of Acts, the resurrected Jesus tells his disciples not to be involved in any ministry because they are not ready for it. Instead, they are to stay put and wait until they, "receive power when the Holy Spirit comes." (1:4, 8) You see, the heart of the Christian message is not *information* about God, but actually Christ himself through the Holy Spirit, who comes with the power to set people free and restore broken lives. Genuinely *Christian* ministry—missions, preaching, evangelism, caring for your neighbor, leading Sunday school, providing for needs, serving, modeling Jesus for your family, all these kinds of things—is not about method or skill. Fundamentally, ministry is not even about passing along the right information about God. It's about sharing Christ himself, who is only rightly communicated if I allow him to express himself in me.

Ministry is not a technique, it is the expression in words or actions of the reality of the Christ life in you and in me, of something that has happened and is happening in your and my own life. The ability to serve God can't be learned by practice or by taking a course. Effective service like this is only ever the result of a life that has been supernaturally changed from the inside. When Christ moves in through the Holy Spirit, life looks different. That's when real ministry happens.

## What does it mean to be sanctified?

So what does it mean to *be* sanctified? I think it means something like becoming 'best friends' with God. What I mean is this. It isn't hard to see that there are some people in my life that are friends—good friends, for whom I am deeply thankful—but some others that are truly *best* friends, friends no matter what. For me, sanctification means having that kind of deep, open, unconditional friendship with God. Doesn't that seem like what Moses experienced, when "inside the Tent of Meeting, the LORD would speak to Moses face to face, as one speaks to a friend"? (Ex 33:11) Or consider Abraham, who James says "was even called a friend of God." (2:23; or Isa 41:8) Becoming a Christian means becoming friends with God—genuinely friends—but sanctification involves that something more which transforms an ordinary friendship into a 'best-friendship'.

When I think of my best friends, with a couple I can pin down pretty precisely when our ordinary friendship took that big step forward, but with a couple others, it just seems to have happened and I can't exactly say when. But ultimately, how the 'best-friendship' began is of a much smaller importance than how it continues. I think that describes the pretty widely varying experience of sanctification of Christians I know. Some can point to a specific moment when God moved in, and some cannot, or maybe only to a particular season in life. I fear that if we only ask about the beginnings of the sanctified life, we are asking the wrong question. Jesus never says you can tell a tree by asking about when it was planted, he says "you can identify a tree by its fruit." (Mt 7:20)

The concept of 'best-friendship with God' further helps me to hold the pieces of the doctrine of sanctification together better. If sanctification is a best-friendship, it makes it a lot less cumbersome to understand how sanctification is both a crisis (something that happens all at once) and a process (something that happens a little at a time). That feels to me just how a best-friendship comes to be: if my best-friendships are deeper today, that doesn't mean they were worse before. I was best-friends, I still am, but the best-friendship itself has grown (or even surged!) in a way that doesn't take any-thing away from the way it was in the past. Moreover, being best friends with God gives me great security. With a best friend, you know you are always loved, and always welcome, even if you have botched it. You can work things out with a best friend, even when you have somehow done them wrong. The assurance of our salvation will always remain fragile if it is not grounded in a rich experience of sanctification, of being best friends with God. (Jn 10:27-28; Ro 8:38-39)

When I was at seminary I read a little book called *The Life of Moses* by Gregory of Nyssa and it significantly im-pacted my perspective on the deeper life. Gregory wrote that:

> This is true perfection: not to avoid a wicked life be-cause like slaves we servilely fear punishment, nor to do good because we hope for rewards, as if cashing

in on the virtuous life by some business-like and contractual arrangement. On the contrary, disregarding all those things for which we hope and which have been reserved by promise, we regard falling from God's friendship as the only thing dreadful and we consider becoming God's friend the only thing worthy of honor and desire.

Where does our holiness come from? Why are we obedient? Fear? Hope of reward? No; the roots of true holiness run deeper than that. John says that "those who obey God's word truly show how completely they love him." (1J 2:5) The root of obedience is the love of a friend. We are holy because we are like him, in the way that a friend is like friend. We follow him—we live our lives God's way—because we love him as a best friend. Our holiness is not itself our friendship with God, but it is one of the real results of that friendship. We obey, and we cut the things that hurt him out of our lives, because our friendship with him is more important than our freedom to do it on our own. Perfection in life doesn't mean never getting it wrong, it means living our lives as best friends with God. That's what I think it means to be sanctified.

### *If I was preparing for accreditation I would . . .*
- Memorize I Thessalonians 5:23, Colossians 1:27, and Acts 1:8
- Read the first ten, and especially the last five, pages of Gregory of Nyssa's excellent and unique book, *The Life of Moses*

- Be ready to talk about what sanctification looks like in my life
- Download and listen to "Break Every Chain" by Jesus Culture

# 14. The Church

## *What is the Church?*

As everyone already knows, the thing that really makes the Church the Church is not the building. That doesn't mean that the building is always extraneous. Church buildings are powerful cultural symbols declaring the presence of the kingdom of God in our communities: they offer outsiders, and insiders, a clear, physical location where the gospel can be found and a place to turn to in a time of crisis or in beginning the search for God. Church buildings help make the gospel—in the hands of church people: us Christians—easier to find. Moreover, church buildings help to shape our histories as families, as the place where the significant stages of our lives have been marked. Our births, weddings, and deaths and those of our loved ones are tied together into one story of God at work among us in part because those events—and many others—are celebrated in this place and as a part of the community that hangs out together here. Finally, church buildings, at their best, also provide space for the non-utilitarian part of our existence. What I mean is this. A church building is different than a bank or a mall in that it doesn't have to be put to maximum use to be really effective. In fact, if we find that our church buildings are operating in a way that is purely functional, even very effectively so, that probably means they are falling short of all that they could be and are failing to be all that they ought to be for us. (The same could probably be said of our pastors too.) A church building is supposed to be the kind of place where we can escape from the rest of our life in modern society, a life where we are always pushed to get the most return on the least investment. On the contrary, a church building should be a place that has different kinds of goals: worship, restoration, prayer, fellowship, relax, eternity. Especially in the city, almost all of life has been secularized; our church buildings are one of the few remaining places we have that we can make genuinely sacred, devoted to time spent with God and with one another in a way that doesn't have to be maximized to be 'worth it'.

Church buildings are fantastic, they are important, but they are not the Church.

So, what is the Church? The Church is not the church building; it's the people. The Church is the body of Christ, and Christ himself is the head.

Of course the Bible uses many word pictures to talk about the Church, but the most common is this one, that we are the real physical presence of Christ in the world, operating together as one body. *His* body. Paul says it most clearly: "You are the body of Christ," he writes to the Corinthians, "and each one of you is part of it." (1Co 12:27) The Church does not merely originate with Christ, in a significant way the Church itself *is* the tangible expression of Jesus Christ. And so, because we are his body, the best way for us to understand who, corporately, we are supposed to be and how we are to engage the world around us is to look at who Jesus Christ was and how he engaged society when he himself was present among us in the body. The Church's chief task is to be for the world in this day and age what the physical Christ was to it back then because, today, we are that body.

The body of Christ, therefore, is one thing, not many things. It is not even merely the compilation of many things all grouped together. We, like Jesus, are not the result of the assembly of a bunch of various parts. Remember: Jesus was conceived as a single human in the womb of his mother Mary and was born and grew and died as the inhabitant of one body. Likewise, the Church, fundamentally, is *one* thing. This is the primary reason why it is inadequate to think of the Church simply as the collection of all the Christians either in one local place or even throughout all of history. The Church's essence is not a heap of individuals; the Church is the super-naturally constituted body of Christ in the world. Christ makes the Church exist. We individual Christians become members of the body as we are made members of Christ by God's power, but we ourselves never make the body the body by gathering together in one place. The Church's reality is grounded not upon you and me, but upon Christ himself, who is our head. The Church, the body, is one.

And of course right now it is shattered into pieces in all kinds of ways, and its broken-apart-ness seems impossible for us to overcome. That's one of the reasons why every pastor should read Oscar Cullmann's book *A Message to Catholics and Protestants*, not because it is a perfect book or that Cullmann's proposal is the best of which we could possibly conceive. Not at all. Rather, Cullmann is remarkable because he honestly faces the divisions of the Church and admits that he thinks it is impossible to overcome them, but then he also confesses that these divisions are wrong, that they go against the grain of the New Testament and God's plan for the Church, and then decides that he is going to be the kind of pastor who always works for the unity of the body of Christ, even in the face of the impossible task. We are limited; we know that we cannot simply hold hands and unite all the churches together. That would be a disaster. We especially cannot unite together by abandoning our commitment to the truth of the gospel in the search for common ground, as some have tried in the past. But we can be men and women who recognize that Christ has only one body, that at the end of the age there will be only one bride of God the Son, and spend our lives working to make that future hope a reality in the present wherever God gives us the opportunity. The body of Christ is one body, not many.

As the one body, the Church is the primary plan by which God makes himself present to the world. Just as Jesus in his earthly life was called Immanuel, 'God with us', so too the Church is God with us: God himself, reaching out in love to the world in a way that can be touched and felt and experienced. Whenever the Church fails to make the presence of God real in the society around it, it begins to fail to truly be the Church. Like Christ, a central part of the purpose of having a body is to bring the presence of God into the world—into the midst of the lost—in a tangible way. The Church *is* the body of Christ.

And it is not always beautiful. The Bible says that neither was Jesus, although of course in his case we mean a lack of physical attractiveness, not the ugliness of sin that we can often see in the Church. But there is a parallel. When he became incarnate, Christ never gave up his identity as the eternal Son of God, and yet his whole earthly life was limited to one location, one time, and all the limitations—the strengths and weaknesses—that come with having a human body. It is the same with his body the Church. Like the incarnate Christ, the identity of the Church is universal—stretching across places and times—but its expression is particular. The local church is no less *really* the Church, *really* the true body of Christ, than the local Jesus Christ in Palestine is *really* the true Son of God, in spite of all his particularities. Being Christ's body means being both universal *and* local, expansive *and* particular.

This has meaning for me and my family too, as church members. In one sense, our membership is membership in Christ, in his universal body. But in another sense, just like the incarnate Jesus, there is no other body of Christ for us than the particular expression of the local Church. Besides all the pragmatic reasons—especially decision making, being committed to one another, and submitting to the direction and discipline of our leaders—we choose to be members of the local church because in doing so we declare our membership in the body of Christ, cosmically considered. I don't have a universal family, I have a particular one: I need a particular church. That's the place where my identity with the universal Christ finds local expression. I know that in some places church membership has been so cheapened that it seems to have almost no content; in this case, what others do doesn't dissuade me. I am a local church member because the local church really is the body of Christ.

Further, as members together of one body, in a very real

way we make each other who we are as the Church. No one part of the body is autonomous. Rather, each one contributes to making all of the parts together actually be a body, constituted with Christ as our head and our life. Sharing life together is a necessary part of being the Church because the Church was specially brought into being by Christ and bears the marks of his own Trinitarian life and craftsmanship. (Mt 16:18) The substance of the Church is a reflection of the substance of the Son, who its source and head. Remember: the essence of God the Son is not something that he possesses outright on his own; his substance—his being, or *ousia*—is the relationship of love that he shares with the Father and the Spirit. Three persons, one substance. This life of God is reflected in the Church. Each of us is a part, but none of us, or even some group of us, possess the *essence* of the Church on our own: the substance of the Church is our relationship together, and that of all of us together with Christ, our head. Not just the substance of the Church as a whole, but *my* substance as a church member: we make each other who we are. Many members, one body. The Church has substance not because we each individually bring a little bit and, pooled together, we have enough for Church. The Church is real because we mutually offer ourselves to one another in the presence of God.

There are two implications of this. First, the size of our local churches is not important, but the mutual love of the members is. The particular expression of the universal body of Christ can be big or small; what makes it the real Church is the way that its members offer themselves to one another in love, and together offer themselves to Christ. Being the

Church is not achieved by accumulation, but by intensity of mutual love. Second, we should never let ourselves forget about members of our body who aren't often present, because they too are a part of what defines us together as the body. There are some people who—on account of work schedule, sickness, travel, missions, or a lot of other reasons—don't get seen very often in our services. Don't forget them. I think that this is part of the meaning of corporate prayer, the very personal activity of declaring before God that this or that person is part of what makes us the Church, that we are not complete without them, and asking God's favor and presence for them in their sickness or work or mission or whatever, just as we ask for God's favor and presence on the rest of us gathered all together. Dear Lord God, that one, that friend, is a part of us, a part of me, a part of the same body, please care for them too this day, I am not the same without them.

The Church is the body of Christ, and so it looks like Christ.

It is also, of course, like Christ in the way that it acts. It constantly gives glory to God the Father through obedience— holiness—and through worship. It socializes and enjoys God's good creation, including the company of tax collectors and sinners. It is ready to suffer. It cares about, and works to meet, the physical needs of the people around it, and it espe- cially cares about the spiritual needs of the lost. (Here we see how both missions and social action are not only required of the Church, but flow from the same source: care for others in Christ's name.) The Church acts in the way that Christ acts by proclaiming as clearly as it can the Good News of the forgiveness of sins, power over evil and death in the world (and in my life), and the arrival of God's glorious kingdom—it preaches, teaches, evangelizes, and disciples. It is a shepherd both to the flock that God gives it and to the lost sheep that it extends itself to seek out and rescue. It stands ready to receive the insults of the world, but prays for God's intervention to forgive the sinner and to change the world through its agency. The Church works out the plan of God for the world in a tangible way. The Church is the body of Christ.

By way of conclusion, a note to pastors. The Church is the body of Christ, but it is also his bride. And he's in love. Part of what it means to be the pastor is to be a part of preparing the Church for the final glorious wedding: encouraging her in holiness, in evangelism, in understanding, and in readiness for the return of Christ the bridegroom. But also, like a best friend at the wedding, as church leaders we need to learn to *love* the bride just like Christ does, even if she sometimes makes us crazy and we have no idea why he chose her.

I probably read 2 Corinthians 11:28 dozens of times before I ever really appreciated what it was actually about. (I even memorized it Bible quizzing!) Paul, after listing all his troubles—like being beaten with rods, imprisoned, and shipwrecked—writes that "besides all this, I have the daily burden of my concern for all the churches." How is that possible? How is 'concern for the churches' more serious than jail or starvation? For me, I never understood this verse until I became assistant pastor at a broken church and God taught me how to love the church like he loves it, the kind of love that rips you apart inside to think about all the grief it faces and how deeply you just want to see it succeed and flourish in the joy of life with God. God's heart breaks when he sees hurting churches—and when he sees hurting people—and so he gives his pastors, his shepherds, the burden of sharing that love for his people, the kind of love Christ has for his bride. If you want to be a great pastor, one of the things you can do is memorize 2 Corinthians 11:28 and, when you pray for your church, pray that God will give you that kind of love, along with the strength to stand up under the weight of it. If we learn to love the Church like that, even though we will continue to make mistakes, I genuinely believe we will never go far wrong in helping to guard and prepare it for the day when Christ comes again and claims his bride, claims us, brimming with that same, amazing love.

### *If I was preparing for accreditation I would . . .*

- Memorize 1 Corinthians 12:27 along with 2 Corinthians 11:28 and Matthew 16:18
- Read *A Message to Catholics and Protestants* by Oscar Cullmann, at least pages 11-19, and 26-36
- Be aware that sometimes in theological writing the word 'Church' is spelled with an upper-case 'C' to talk about the Church at all times and in all places, and is spelled with a lower-case 'c' to talk about the local church or about just one segment of the church.

# 15. Communion and Baptism

*Why are communion and baptism important?*

In many ways, this world that we live in is a truly lonely and hard place. People, even sometimes the people we most trust or rely on, abandon or disappoint us; they are taken from us by death or sometimes just simply move on. Our favorite places slowly fall apart and fail to be what they once were to us. And patterns of life to which we have grown accustomed sharply change and we realize that we cannot continue to live in their familiarity any longer. In many ways, adult life is a slow process of accommodating ourselves to a world that is increasingly strange and unfamiliar, where the things we knew and loved, even ourselves, age and change and waste away.

That's why communion and baptism are important, because they are tangible signs of the unchangeableness of God's plan in the midst of lives so burdened with change and death that sometimes we feel nearly crushed by the weight. Communion and baptism are the place where God has promised us he will always be for us, in the same way he always has been, bearing with him the full availability of his gentle love that we saw once at our conversion but sometimes feels so far away. Communion and baptism are important because they are a special and precious place where God has promised to always make himself available to us.

The theological word for these two places, the places where God has promised to meet us in a special way, is *'sacrament'*. When we call communion and baptism sacraments, we mean four main things: they are a physical ritual, they nevertheless carry a deep spiritual significance, they have been instituted by Jesus himself, and they make a difference in our lives because God works in them through his Holy Spirit.

First, then, the sacraments are physical. You see, God understands very clearly that we cannot always make our 'feelings' do what we want. He, in Jesus Christ, has himself experienced real human feelings, just like ours. God knows that our memories are frail, and how easy it is, when we are discouraged or alone, to doubt the things of which we were once so sure. It's why he gave us physical baptism, and why he made it something that always includes other people as witnesses. When I am on the bottom, I can forget the feelings I had the day that Jesus came into my life, or maybe even talk myself into doubting that I've ever really been saved at all, but I cannot doubt that my baptism happened. Not that my baptism saves me, God does. But because my baptism is something physical—something I can point back to without the dispute of my memory—God can use it to give me courage in the face of spiritual self doubt or the attack of the devil. In the same way, communion is a physical activity on account of the fact that God understands the frailty of our psyches. Sometimes I cannot make my heart feel 'worshipful' or 'spiritual', even though I very genuinely want to. God knows that. And so he has made it so that even when I cannot make myself 'feel' anything when I worship, even when prayer is difficult and my spiritual life seems so cold, I can come to God in communion, and find him there. Communion is a meal and not an exercise in 'thinking spiritual thoughts' because God knows that sometimes that's all we're really capable of, and he loves us enough to want us around even when that's all we can give. The sacraments are physical.

Second, the sacraments are also spiritual. In communion, we receive God's special spiritual grace of forgiveness, are given afresh a special opportunity to repent of life lived 'not God's way', and are brought back together into the unity of God's family. In Old Testament times, the head of the family would go to sacrifice the offering at the temple, but the meat would be brought home for everyone to eat. By participating in that meal they participated in the offering and claimed its validity in their own lives even though they were not present when it was sacrificed. The same is true for us. We were not there when Christ was sacrificed for our sins, but when we eat the bread and drink the cup in faith God freely and graciously applies the offering of Christ afresh to each one of us. From our perspective, communion is the opportunity that God gives us to say once again: 'Heavenly Father, that sacrifice of Jesus Christ that happened so long ago, I need it once again today, and, in faith and repentance, I claim it once more for me and for my family.' Because we share together in this one sacrifice—even though we were not present with Christ there and are not always present to one another here—God creates real spiritual unity among us through communion. Paul says that "though we are many, we all eat from one loaf of bread, showing that we are one body." (1Co 10:17) In communion, God *makes* us family in a special way, as we commune with him and with one another.

Likewise, in baptism we receive God's special grace of welcome into his family. If conversion is the place where we are reborn, baptism is the place where we are re-named as a member of God's family. Because we are one family, we are all baptized into the same name of God the Father, God the Son, and God the Spirit. In doing so, God claims us in a special way as his own children, just as my children bear not just my features and my likeness, but also formally carry my name. And just as it would seem bizarre to wait years before filling out the birth certificate application for a newborn and finalizing his membership in the family by giving him the family name, it ought to seem bizarre to us to wait years between conversion and baptism in our churches. Communion is the sacrament of forgiveness afresh; baptism is the sacrament of welcome into God's family. Neither is merely a physical symbol; both bring God's grace into our lives in an unseen but tremendously real way. The sacraments are spiritual.

Third, the sacraments are the only two parts of Christian worship given to us directly by Jesus Christ. Right from the start, in both the New Testament and in the earliest church, Christian worship contained many of the elements that still characterize it today: preaching, meeting together in a regular place, singing, reading the Bible, praying, socializing together, and collecting an offering. All of these are biblical and important aspects of our Christian identity, but even above these stand communion and baptism because the Bible so clearly points out how they are the commands of Jesus himself. "Go," says Jesus, "and make disciples of all the nations, baptizing them in the name of the Father and the Son and the

Holy Spirit." (Mt 28:19) "This is my body," he says at the last supper, "which is given for you. Do this to remember me." (1Co 11:24) Even if we don't always understand everything that communion and baptism mean, they are a non-negotiable part of how we structure worship in our churches because it was Jesus himself who gave them to us. The sacraments are important because Jesus teaches us that this is how we ought to worship, this is where we can expect to find him when we come together to celebrate and to commemorate the salvation he won for us on the cross.

Finally, communion and baptism are meaningful for us because God himself gives them meaning by his Holy Spirit. The bread and the cup and the water are not the real thing. God is the real thing, and the spiritual grace of the sacraments comes to us only because God himself comes to us through them. Not that he cannot work in other ways, or is not present at other times, but he has put these two activities into the very center of our Christian lives as places where, above all others, he offers himself to be found. It's a little like trying to find me at work if you have an appointment to come by 'in the afternoon'. Sometimes I'll be in the library, sometimes in class, sometimes in the computer lab, sometimes out for a walk to get a snack (or a break), sometimes in the lobby chatting, and sometimes at the registrar's. You might find me by looking in any of those places, but if you go to my office, and wait, you will eventually always find me there. In fact, it would be confusing to me if you didn't always start your search for me there, because that is the place where I already told you I would plan to meet with you. God is like that, but in a sense that is more true and more just. He is in all these places, but especially in the place where he has already said that he will meet us: in communion and in baptism. The sacraments are important because they are where God stands ready to meet with us in a special way. They are important because God is present to us in the midst of them through the Holy Spirit.

This of course means that quarreling over the physical parts of communion and baptism—crackers or bread, juice or wine, one big cup or lots of little cups, sprinkling or immersing—is an offense to God himself, because it suggests that God is only able to be present if we get the physical symbols exactly right. The truth of course is that none of us probably ever get the symbols right, if 'right' means doing it precisely the way that Jesus did it. Thank God that when it comes to the sacraments doing it exactly how Jesus did it is the least important thing. Even if the person who baptized you turns out in the end to have been an idol worshiper all along, your baptism is still true baptism (which is, by and large, the story of the 'Donatist controversy'). The sacraments are effective at bringing God's presence into our lives in a special way because nothing can stand in the way of God accomplishing his will-to-love, not because of the correctness of the symbols, the purity of our pastors, or even how well we have managed to perfectly recreate the experience of Jesus and his first disciples. Communion and baptism have power in our lives because of the Holy Spirit, not because of how we 'do' them. "Water," says Peter, "is a picture of baptism, which now saves you, not by removing dirt from your body, but as a response to God from a clean conscience. It is effective because of the resurrection of Jesus Christ."

(1P 3:21) The sacraments are real because God himself is the one who makes them real by coming and being present to us through his Holy Spirit.

A few weeks ago my family and I were in church together and, after taking communion, my son caught my attention and, eyes twinkling, rubbed his tummy and whispered to me: "I really needed something like that." Of course he meant that he had been hungry for a snack, which I in fact also was, but he also somehow managed to express the essence of why communion and baptism are important in just a few words. 'I really needed something like that.'

I needed a physical reminder—like a badge—of my salvation that I could refer back to. I needed a tangible activity that I could participate in when my heart felt 'cold' or 'blank' when I came to worship. I needed something to re-make me into one family with my brother and sister Christians. I needed forgiveness this week, I needed a chance to repent again and get a fresh start again from God's hand. I needed what Ignatius called the "medicine of immortality, and the antidote to prevent us from dying," to re-infuse the health of the risen Christ into my life after a week of everything that this week has been. I needed to be connected with the real, tangible life that Jesus lived and the things that he taught. I needed the actual presence of God in my life.

Communion and baptism are important because they represent the place where, in spite of everything that goes on in and all around us, God promises to meet us with the power of the risen Christ, offering his grace in a special way through the personal presence of his Holy Spirit. And I really needed something like that.

*If I was preparing for accreditation I would . . .*

- Read "The Ministry of Baptism and Eucharist", in Thomas Oden's book, *Pastoral Theology*, chapter eight (105-126)
- Understand the meaning of the terms 'sacrament' and 'Eucharist'
- Memorize Matthew 28:19, 1 Corinthians 11:23-26, and 1 Corinthians 10:17

# 16. Suffering

*How would you begin to explain suffering within the*
*Church or in the life of the Christian?*

For Christians, just like for everybody else, the question of suffering is a difficult one. We can talk about it; in fact, as Christian people, that is certainly one of the things we ought to be able to do. But even as much as we think about it, and as much as we talk it through, suffering remains one of the ultimately unexplainable parts of our lives. Not 'unexplainable' in the brutish sense, where we think about all of our experiences simply as the depressing consequences of living in a totally random and ungoverned universe, and where we each therefore try to make the best of it by choosing to say that the life the cosmos has forced on me is the life I am going to decide to live the best I can (which is, give or take, the philosophy of *existentialism*). As Christians, we believe that life isn't something shoved at us that we have to learn how to deal with, but the good gift of a loving Father who created us with a plan. And so our difficulty isn't trying to find meaning in an otherwise meaningless existence, but trying to explain how the suffering we do experience could possibly fit into that plan.

Because it seems clear that suffering *is* somehow included as a part of God's plan for his people, part of what he allows to happen; it certainly was for Jesus and for his earliest followers. With the exception of John (who died in exile) and Judas (who betrayed him), all of Jesus' original disciples, and of course Jesus himself, were eventually executed. Paul, likewise, taught that "everyone who wants to live a godly life in Christ Jesus will suffer persecution." (2Ti 3:12) That was the experience of the earliest church. Not only were they brutally persecuted physically, but for hundreds of years they found themselves as social outsiders on account of their new, counter-cultural religious beliefs. And so it comes as no surprise that the suffering of the people of God is one of the major themes of the New Testament. In the West, although the Church is often mocked or ostracized, it is not persecuted as it once was, but throughout the rest of the world it still is: churches are bombed or shut down, pastors are stabbed, young Christian converts are poisoned by their own family members, and people's livelihoods are destroyed. The Church still suffers at the hands of the world.

But we also know, don't we, that you don't have to be persecuted to very genuinely suffer. We know that Christians get sick, Christians get stressed, and Christians lose their jobs. We know that some Christians have been abused, or wrongly treated in deeply hurtful ways, that some have had to bear deep and painful secrets alone, and we have seen our own friends in the church go through all kinds of impossibly difficult circumstances. We know from experience that Christians are included alongside everyone else when our communities experience tragedy or unexpected economic or natural catastrophes, that Christians fail at achieving their dreams and live with long term disappointment, and that, just like everybody, else Christians sometimes go through horrible difficulties in their relationships and at work. More than that even, sometimes we Christians hurt each other. Even inside the Church. Even in the process of ministry. Ask any pastor: life in the church, though filled with hope on account of Jesus Christ, is a life that involves every kind of sorrow and suffering. This is part of the very reason why God has given the church pastors, so that there is always someone available to speak the care and love of God, in a tangible and visible way, into the deep and real grief that arises in the life of every church community. If you are a pastor or elder or small group leader, never forget that a part of your responsibility is to take the suffering that happens in your church seriously, and to grieve and suffer alongside those who are faced with fiery trials.

Going through suffering doesn't mean being an inadequate Christian, it means being a normal one. Peter, who himself was crucified by Emperor Nero, wrote to the churches saying: "Dear friends, don't be surprised at the fiery trials you are going through, as if something strange were happening to you. Instead, be very glad—for these trials make you partners with Christ in his suffering, so that you will have the wonderful joy of seeing his glory when it is revealed to all the world." (1P 4:12-13) This doesn't mean that we jump with joy when troubles come, but just that we understand hard times not as a kind of cruel meaninglessness like some do, nor as some random happening we could have avoided had we been luckier. No; suffering, in all the various and vicious ways that it comes, is a normal part of the Christian life.

Sometimes it can be tempting to promote Christianity—

both to ourselves and to others—as a way to escape all the troubles of life. It is not. Becoming a Christian means deliverance: from Sin and eternal death and from the fear of the dark powers in the world. And becoming a Christian means blessing: we have the presence of God the Holy Spirit always with us, we have the security of eternal life to come, we have supernatural power from God to break free from our old way of living and to be set free from addiction and self harm, we have the guidance of the Bible and of the Church to help us steer our lives in God's way, and we have God's special miraculous power to heal and to miraculously change circumstances which sometimes breaks into our lives as a foretaste of the life to come. Most importantly of all, being a Christian means having hope, even if we cannot explain in words all that we are going through. But Christianity does not mean escaping the normal, hard sufferings that come with being a human, and it does not mean being guaranteed a better or more comfortable life. Being a child of God's promise does not mean that if we have faith things will always go our way, or even go our way more often (which is the root idea of the 'prosperity gospel' movement). That certainly isn't what Christ or his disciples experienced. Sometimes, being a Christian means *more* suffering, not less.

But why? Why doesn't God rescue us? All of us, all humanity, but especially us, his children? Especially me, and my family, and the ones that I love so much; if God cares so much, why does he not step in *my* life?

Why? That's the question that makes suffering unexplainable. Because we know that God indeed does care. The Psalmist says to God: "You keep track of all my sorrows. You have collected all my tears in your bottle. You have recorded each one in your book." (Ps 56:8) Our suffering does not go unnoticed by God, or unrecorded. He knows every wrong that we have endured. And in fact we believe that at the end of time, when Jesus comes again he will make things right and somehow take away all the hurt and damage that we have received over the course of our lives. That will maybe be his greatest miracle, to somehow overcome all the sorrow and suffering accumulated throughout human history. It certainly stands at the very center of our Christian hope. God cares. But why does he wait? Why does he not step in right now and stop suffering from happening, especially in the Church? That's the question we need to try our best to understand, and the one we ought never to let ourselves stop asking.

There are three main reasons why God allows suffering to be a normal part of being a Christian.

## Suffering and God's discipline

Sometimes, suffering in the life of a Christian person is the result of the discipline of God, in both senses of the word 'discipline'. On the one hand, God disciplines us to train us or to help us develop. Just like an endurance runner who increases their mileage little by little each week, sometimes God lets the hard things in our life continue, and maybe even get gradually harder and harder, so that we will be strong enough to face the next big project that he has for us. On the other hand, sometimes God disciplines us in response to our own disobedience, or our unwillingness to live our life according to his good plan. God doesn't cause the suffering that we encounter, but he genuinely does let it happen, especially when that means letting us feel the consequences of our own bad decisions.

In both cases, suffering because God is disciplining us is difficult, but it does not mean that we are outside his love or outside his plan. Hebrews says that "the LORD disciplines those he loves, and he punishes each one he accepts as his child," and that, "if God doesn't discipline you as he does all of his children, it means that you are illegitimate and are not really his children at all." (Hb 12:6, 8) God sometimes allows suffering in our lives as a part of his plan to make us perfect. Experiencing God's discipline doesn't mean we are about to somehow 'lose our salvation', it means the opposite. It means that he loves us and that we have a secure place in his family. Suffering as a Christian is in fact one of the grounds of the assurance of our salvation. The Lord disciplines those he loves. And of course, "no discipline is enjoyable while it is happening—it's painful! But afterward there will be a peaceful harvest of right living for those who are trained in this way. . . . God's discipline is always good for us, so that we might share in his holiness." (Hb 12:10-11)

It is not correct to interpret *all* suffering as the discipline of God. Particularly when we look at the lives of others, we need to be extra careful to not automatically explain away the pain that they are going through as simply part of some 'bigger plan'. But sometimes the hurt that we experience in life is the result of God's discipline. I've seen it in my own life. In 2006 I experienced what was for me a total catastrophe when my examiners asked for a year's worth of corrections to my doctoral thesis. I didn't know how I could possibly move forward. I felt like my whole life had been turned upside-down; my self-confidence was broken to bits. It was horrible, and I was in bad shape for a long time. But as I was working through it all God met me one day and gave me Psalm 118:18 as a way of saying, "Ben, I need you to be someone different than you are right now." And so I've ended up as maybe the only Christian with Psalm 118:18 as a life verse: "The LORD has punished me severely, but he did not let me die." God stills sometimes explains my life to me that way. Letting me go through one of the worst years ever didn't happen because God wanted to ruin me or because he had stopped loving; it meant the opposite. God loved me and I had a secure place in his family, but he needed to make some changes in my heart to help me become who he wanted me to be right now. Sometimes, not always, but sometimes, the suffering we go through is the result of the discipline of God.

## Suffering and being the body of Christ

To understand the second reason why there is suffering in the Church, we have to take a quick look backward to our understanding of who God is. Remember, God himself is the God whose Triune love overflows in his creation: God created because he loves us. And his love is *real* love, the kind of love that can be declined, not something that is ever forced upon us. This is why, against everything we would count as common sense, God placed the tree of the knowledge of good and evil right in the center of the garden. Rather than using his position of power and majesty to pressure a response of love from us, God planned that we should always have a clear opportunity to not love him back, to choose not to be his friend. And, as we know, that is in fact what we chose.

It's the same reason why God placed Israel in the midst of the nations, and why Jesus came in a human flesh that could be not only seen and touched, but cut and abused. Because God really loves, God makes his offer of love easy to find, and equally easy to reject. Those who seek him can find him, and those also that want to lash out at him in anger are able to do that too. These two themes always go together: God's love is proclaimed by his servant, and God opens himself up to the rejection of the world through the rejection of his servant.

The Church suffers for the same reason. It suffers because God has placed it in the middle of the world both to proclaim his message of salvation and to be the tangible place where the world can shake its fist at God when it wants to reject him.

The suffering of the Church is the sign to the world that God's love is real love, love that can be accepted *or* rejected. The Church suffers because it stands before the world as God's servant—as the body of Christ himself—and takes all the abuse that the world wants to hurl at God.

This is why when Jesus confronts Paul, who was on his way to Damascus to persecute the church there, he says, "Saul, Saul, why are you persecuting me?" (Ac 9:4) Not 'why are you persecuting my people?', but 'why are you persecuting *me*?' To attack the Church is to attack Christ himself and his gospel. The world understands it; God understands it. God set it up that way on purpose, so that it would always be easy to shout 'No!' right in his face, because only then can the 'Yes!' that our hearts sing out to him in faith be counted as the genuine 'Yes!' of real, free love. That was the whole reason he created, to woo us and to share his love. Not that we have the strength to say 'Yes!' all on our own. Of course not; no one thinks that. We are only able to call out to God because he himself makes us able to. But he never forces our 'Yes!', and he never takes away our freedom to say 'No!', which is part of the reason he established the Church. The Church is God's promise to the world that he will never force its love, that he will always remain available for its rejection, because having the chance to say 'No!' is the one thing that gives our 'Yes!' real meaning. Because of Sin, the world is always saying 'No!' to God, and so the Church remains the location of the world's ongoing persecution of Christ.

This is what the apostle Paul is talking about when he says that "I am glad when I suffer for you in my body, for I am participating in the sufferings of Christ that continue for his body, the church." (Col 1:24) The sufferings of Christ continue; he is still being rejected, physically and emotionally, just as he was during his earthly ministry. Then it was his human body that bore the world's rage against him, now it is his body the Church. The Church is abused because the Church really is the body of Christ, and because God has therefore put it in the middle of the garden so that the path away from his love will always remain open and accessible, just as the path back towards him equally always is. The Church suffers because God truly so loves the world, even when it continues to hate him back.

## Suffering and Sin

Finally, and ultimately, suffering both inside and outside the Church is the consequence of sin. Because God loves us, he is patient with us. And so, as we all know, the Church is full of all sorts of people, including the ones who still have a long way to go. Maybe that describes most of us, in one way or another. There ought not to be conflict or sin in the Church—especially not willful sin—but there is, and its effects are brutal, especially when our expectations of other Christians go so unmet and it makes us so frustrated that we just want to shout: "This should not be happening *in the Church*!" But because God is patient, he makes room in his family for each of us. God even makes room for me. That's one of the reasons why there is suffering in the Church, because *I* cause it.

But in a broader sense, most of the suffering we see in the Church, in the lives of our friends, is just an extension of the horrible problem of suffering in the world. We, collectively, suffer because we, collectively, are people who sin. Sometimes God protects us from it, or rescues us in a special way. On a global scale, I am convinced that he *always* limits it—not just for Christians, but for all humanity—and that if we could see the full picture we would be able to understand all the ways that God has planned and intervened to make our world immeasurably better than it otherwise might have been. But most of the time God lets his people go through the same kind of sufferings their non-Christian neighbors do. That's the hardest thing to explain. All that suffering of course starts with the sin of some person, which eventually overflows in hurt and injury to another, sometimes more and sometimes less directly. Suffering comes from sin, and all of us continue to live in the same world, a world flooded with sin. This of course is only the very beginning of an explanation. If we're honest, probably all we can ever really hope to do is to begin.

But remember this. God has a plan, and God is still in control and still with us. He is the God who abandoned the comforts of heaven to come and suffer alongside of us. God knows what it feels like to grieve, and to hurt. God cares about the things that you and I go through, and the things we walk through with the people he has entrusted to us in our ministries. If you are a pastor, or a church leader, remember that our best example in ministry is Jesus, who was not only a dynamic teacher and a great leader, but preeminently a servant who came to suffer: weep and suffer alongside of us and suffer and die on our behalf. That's what it really means to be a pastor. It's what it means to be a Christian, alongside the commitment to fight against sin and suffering in the world wherever we can push it back a little or expend ourselves to rescue our neighbors from it. That's the plan: God has put us in this world for one another.

And if you are suffering right now, remember, God loves you, and God grieves with you. Christians really suffer. Even the ones like the disciples whose lives are marked by vibrant faith and holy living. Don't lose hope. And never forget that God has counted your tears and recorded them in his book. I don't know how he will achieve it—it will be a miracle—but my world only makes sense when I trust that God will one day really will make it right.

***If I was preparing for accreditation I would . . .***

- Memorize Psalm 54:8 and either 1 Peter 4:12-13 or Colossians 1:24
- Read the introduction (pp. 13-26) of John Piper's book *Filling Up the Afflictions of Christ*
- Read *A Tale of Three Kings* by Gene Edwards, especially if I was feeling frustration with other people I was working with in the leadership structure of my own church (I do not recommend Edwards' other books, especially not *The Divine Romance*, but *A Tale of Three Kings* is excellent)

# 17. The Bible

*What are the important elements of a Christian response
to the question: 'What is the Bible?'*

## The Bible is a part of God's plan to reveal himself

The first, and pre-eminent, half of the Christian answer to the question 'what is the Bible' is that the Bible is a part of the plan that God has to reveal himself—his very own self—to us. Remember, God created because he loves us, and wants to invite us into relationship with him. The Bible is a part of that plan. It's not the whole plan of course, but it is a significant part. The Bible, therefore, is much more than a special story or a manual full of information *about* God, it is a place where God himself speaks to us—both individually and together as a Church—and tells us about himself, about his offer of pardon for our sins, and about his invitation to share his love and his company forever in heaven. In the pages of the Bible it is not great men who speak, it is a great God who speaks through them. The Bible is primarily a book about God, just as God planned for it to be.

This is what Peter is talking about when he says that we "must realize that no prophecy in Scripture ever came from the prophet's own understanding, or from human initiative. No, those prophets were moved by the Holy Spirit, and they spoke from God." (2P 1:20-21) Every part of the Bible was written down by human beings like you and me, as we can see even just from how their personalities shine through in their writing style or their favorite words. The Bible was written by people, but people whom God filled and used in a special way, so that the things that they wrote and testified to are really the things that he himself wanted to communicate to us. This is what the word 'inspiration' means in regard to the Scriptures, not that the Bible is 'inspiring' for us, although it is that also, but rather that the words of Scripture are in fact God's own words, given to human authors through the power of the Holy Spirit. God himself is the ultimate author of Scripture, who filled and guided the biblical writers in a unique way so that they could convey the truth of his own being without ever having to stop being real, normal people. All of the Bible is inspired in this way, from the major sweeping themes right down to the very words that were chosen to communicate God's message; because God himself stands behind the Scriptures, there is no part that can be done away with or ignored.

Like all the central themes of Christianity, the inspiration of the Bible is not something that can be proven; it is one of the things that we accept by faith. There are good arguments that can be given in favor of the inspiration of Scripture—especially the fact that the Church still genuinely hears God's voice when it is read—but they do not *prove* that it is true. As the *Apostles' Creed* says: "I believe in the Holy Scriptures." I believe that they really are part of God plan to tell me about his character and to reconcile me and my community to himself. It is in this sense that the Bible is the cornerstone of faith and practice in the Church, because nowhere else does God speak to us with the clarity and the certainty that we find in Scripture. Any evangelical discussion about the Bible must begin by acknowledging that, by the power of God the Holy Spirit, it is a supernatural place where God truly and authoritatively reveals himself to us.

## The Bible is totally trustworthy

The second half of the answer, or at least the broad strokes of it, is the complete trustworthiness of the Bible, which itself has two important aspects. In the first place, trustworthiness means that we believe the Bible is true, that it is *reliable* and will never lead us astray in any of its claims, especially concerning the things that relate to our salvation. For us Christians, this means that the Bible is the unchanging standard by which everything else gets evaluated, and, because we believe it comes from the hand of a reliable and wise God, we believe that the Bible is a reliable guide for our lives in a way that nothing else could be.

We love the Bible because we love the one who reveals himself to us through it. We rely on the Bible because we have learned that it is safe to rely on God, for all of this life and for all of the life to come. He could have done anything to teach us about himself and about his plan for us, but he decided that the Bible, just the way we have it, was what we needed the most. 2 Timothy 3:16 puts it this way, that "all Scripture is inspired by God and is useful to teach us what is true." Because we trust in the goodness and the might of the one who gave it to us, we trust the Bible more than any other resource. This is what the Alliance Statement of Faith means when it quotes the traditional confession that the Bible constitutes "the divine and only rule of Christian faith and practice." When we need to make decisions about what to believe, how to organize the ministries of the Church, or what the Christian life ought to look like, we always give the Bible the final say. Always. Even if it is at odds with 'conventional wisdom'. As God says through Paul: the "foolish plan of God is wiser than the wisest of human plans, and God's weakness is stronger than the greatest of human strength." (1Co 1:25) Saying that the Bible is reliable, then, involves actually relying on it to govern the way that we live. The practical conviction that the Bible is our only reliable foundation for life and ministry, and that God is the reliable giver of it, forms the first half of what is meant by drawing a boundary along the issue of trustworthiness.

The other half of defining the Bible by its trustworthiness means believing in the consistency between the way that God has revealed himself in Scripture and who he really is. Not that the Bible says everything about God that could be said, or that he is limited to being only what we as humans are capable of knowing about him. That's an impossible idea. (Jn 21:25) Rather, it means that even though God is infinite and beyond our comprehension, all the parts of him that we cannot see and that exceed our ability to understand can always be correlated with who he has already shown himself to be in the parts that we have seen and can understand. The God who meets us in the pages of Scripture is the same God who really is: God's true nature is consistent with what we read of him in the Bible. These two aspects—reliability and consistency—form the second half of our answer to the question of what is the Bible: the Bible is the trustworthy self-revelation of a trustworthy God.

## My Bible is the Bible

If you are a pastor or Bible teacher at any level, and you can, you ought to be augmenting your regular English Bible study (which is irreplaceable) by studying the Bible in its original languages. I know it's hard, but the longer you work at it the easier it gets, and there are some things that you can see in Greek or Hebrew that you'd never notice in English, maybe only because reading in a foreign language forces you to go so slowly. Sometimes when I read the Greek New Testament I feel like I have just put my glasses on and can all of sudden see all the same things but so much more clearly. Of course we need to be honest about our abilities too. Most of us are not Don Carson, which is why we probably all ought to buy his book *Exegetical Fallacies* to remind us to never overestimate our facility in biblical languages.

We ought always to include time for study in the Greek New Testament, but we ought never to mention it from the pulpit. At least almost never.

When we use phrases like 'in the Greek this word means . . .' or 'in the original this verb appears in the aorist . . .' we harm our congregation because we reinforce for them the idea that the *true* Bible, the one that is *really* inspired is the Greek, Hebrew, and Aramaic one. But that's not correct. For the people in our churches, the *real* Bible, the *inerrantly inspired* Bible, the Bible through which God the Holy Spirit speaks the true and powerful Word of God directly into their lives, is the imitation-leather NIV that they bring to small group and read with their kids. Never, never say things like 'I disagree with how the NIV (or the NASB, or the ESV) translated . . .' Not because the translations are flawless: they are not, and we're not obliged to say that they are. But at the same time let us never do anything that undermines the confidence our people have in the Word of God, the Bible that they do their devotions in.

So, disagree with the NIV, or the NLT (which is my favorite); that's fine. Think critically about the translations you have available, compare them, and then choose one—*your* favorite—to use consistently in public ministry. Tell your other pastor friends about why you like the one you do, and be ready to talk to interested lay people about the differences between the translations. But never mention it from the pulpit. If God is mighty enough to inspire Paul and then preserve his handwritten text for thousands of years, he is mighty enough to give you and me the right way to express in English what we have gleaned from our studies in Greek without us ever letting on. Remember, your flock will learn as much from you about the Bible by how you treat it as they do by what you say about it. Let them see your confidence in the Holy Spirit's ability to speak to them as they study the Word at home or in their small group, without any special helps or dictionaries, and you will give them a blessing that goes far beyond anything you could prepare for Sunday morning.

What is the Bible? However we understand and teach the truth of Scripture we can never intrude on the space that the individual believer has to say, "*This* Bible, the one that I am reading, by the power of the Holy Spirit, this is the most real Bible there is." The authority of the Bible should never be allowed to rest on the recreation of the 'best text' or the 'best translation' lest millions of Christians—both past and present—be understood to possess only some derivative from the truly inspired Scripture; an evangelical understanding of the Bible is one that always remembers that, by the grace of God, every believer can say: "*My* Bible is *the* Bible: *my* Bible is the true and inspired Word of God, spoken to me and to the World."

### *If I was preparing for accreditation I would . . .*

- Be aware that the phrase 'verbal inspiration' means that even the *words* of Scripture are inspired, not just the main ideas, and that the phrase 'plenary inspiration' means that *all* the parts of Scripture are equally—fully—inspired
- Memorize 2 Timothy 3:16 and 2 Peter 1:20-1
- Buy *Exegetical Fallacies* by Don Carson and keep it on my desk every time I opened my Greek New Testament

# 18. The Accuracy of the Bible

*How would you respond to a friend who had questions*
*regarding the accuracy of the Bible?*

The Bible is true. True in whatever ordinary sense we understand the word 'true'. It comes to us exactly like God wanted it to, and perfectly satisfies the role he planned for it to play in our lives. The Bible doesn't contain anything accidental or mistaken, but only what God himself decided ought to be included. All its parts—the histories, the poetry, the prophecies, the apocalyptic, the narratives, the didactic sections, the divine speech: all of it—are elements that God himself intended for us to read and interpret together. The Church did not choose the Bible, God did. God gave us the Bible; not one of its parts stands outside his control.

The technical term for this idea is 'inerrancy', meaning that God did not make even one error as he stood behind the authors of Scripture and inspired what they said. The Bible is the inerrant Word of God. Everything in the Bible is exactly the way God wanted it to be, without ever accidentally including something he regretted, without misapprehending how it would be treated and transmitted across the millennia, and without making any errors of any kind. We believe that the Bible is the true and authoritative guide for all of life because we believe that God is its ultimate author and believe that God never makes mistakes. He particularly would never intentionally deceive us. The Bible is true.

Besides 'inerrant', another word that is sometimes used when people want to talk about the way that the Bible is totally true is 'infallible', meaning that because it comes to us from the hand of God, it is impossible that the Bible could fail or mislead us. In ordinary language, 'inerrant' and 'infallible' mean basically the same thing: the whole Bible is completely true—it has no errors, no failings—because it comes to us directly by the inspiration of a wise and trustworthy God. In fact, many evangelicals use these terms interchangeably. But these two words also have a more technical meaning, and several decades ago they stood at the very center of a fierce and sometimes cruel debate within evangelicalism regarding how exactly we ought to describe the truth of the Bible. In the midst of the conflict, the word 'infallible' came to be understood to mean that the parts of the Bible that refer to God's saving plan are completely true and authoritative for us, but its other parts probably contain a number of scientific or historical errors. 'Inerrant', conversely, was taken to mean that every part of the Bible was true, including the scientific or historical bits, but only as they were originally written down by the apostles and prophets (this is what the phrase 'in the autographs' means). As a result of this history—our history—'infallible' is no longer the best word to use to use to talk about the truth of the Bible, even if you mean it in its ordinary sense that 'the Bible doesn't have a single fault'. If that is the idea you want to convey, you should use the word 'inerrant', like the Alliance Statement of Faith rightly does. This doesn't mean that we interpret every element of Scripture, including things such as the clearly apocalyptic or poetic sections, with a sort of cold literalism. Far from it. Believing in inerrancy means working just as hard as anyone else to be sensitive to language, genre, context, intent, and all the other factors which shape our understanding of the text. Rather, using the word 'inerrancy' is a way of standing together to say that we believe without any reservations that the *whole* of the Bible comes from the hand of God, and that we therefore trust it to say exactly what he wanted to say in just the way he wanted to say it. The Bible is the trustworthy self-revelation of a trustworthy God. All of it.

## Just the Bible God wanted us to have

The Bible is perfect. Of course, it's not always perfectly what *we* want it to be: sometimes we want more information about some issue, or wish that some parts of it were written more clearly or more explicitly. Personally, I'd take a hundred more chapters about God's mighty victories in battle to read to my son and at least a hundred more vignettes about brave women and girls of faith for my daughter. It's not always perfectly what we want it to be, but it is always perfect in the sense that it is precisely the thing God wanted it to be. Because he is a good Father, God knows what is best for his children, and because he is mighty we know that the Bible he has actually given us is just the Bible he wanted us to have.

The Bible is also not always perfectly what we expect that it ought to be, and many people have serious and honest concerns about 'problems' within the Bible. Sometimes we ourselves do. This is an important issue for us to be ready to discuss because there *are* 'problems' in the Bible. There *are* small differences between the ancient manuscripts: it is undeniable. Though there is no disunity of theme, there *is* a lack of uniformity to the synoptic Gospels, in both order and, sometimes, content. (Explaining this was one of the questions in *my* ordination exam.) There *are* scientific and historical statements in the Bible that seem a lot easier to explain within the pre-scientific worldview of the ancient world. And in a few places there *are* verses that we cannot understand at all, or even guarantee that we are translating correctly.

Answering questions about the accuracy of the Bible shouldn't mean denying these kinds of issues, it should mean talking about them. But when we do so, we need to remember that God's goal for the Bible was never simply for it to be a manual full of information, but rather the supremely personal communication of his very own self to us, by witnessing to the history of the community he brought into being, the story of his mighty words and actions among them, and the inspired interpretation and instruction he provided to give meaning to the events of that history and to the story of those mighty acts. The Bible looks the way it does because God himself has given it that shape as a part of designing it for a specific purpose. God's intent was to teach us ordinary humans about himself through the Bible, and so he planned that it would be comprehensible in its original context, understandable to ordinary readers, transferable between cultures and languages, communicated by real human authors, and, most important of all, sufficient for our salvation.

You see, God never wanted us to have the Bible and then just stop there; his plan was that through the Bible we would come to know *him* and accept his great invitation: grace, forgiveness, salvation, perfection, glorification, and life forever in his presence. The Bible was never the whole plan; it is an irreplaceable part of it, but the Bible itself is not the goal. God is the goal, and the Bible is his premeditated self-revelation to us; its perfection lies in communicating just what God wanted it to so that we would hear his voice calling to us from its pages. The Bible is perfect, because God—its ultimate author—is perfect. He could have given us anything, but in his eternal wisdom he chose *this* Bible, the one the Church actually has, exactly in all the ways we find it, because it was just the thing he wanted us to have. And he chose to do it this way even in spite of knowing beforehand that sometimes the books of the Old and New Testaments would fail to meet our expectations for how a Bible really ought to look, and even in spite of the fact that we would probably have set it all up a little differently if *we* had been in charge. Mind you, we would have chosen a different kind of Messiah too.

So, if I was asked by a friend about the accuracy of the Bible, these are the themes that I would want to talk through. I know there are 'problems', but their existence doesn't ever make me feel overwhelmed. They certainly never make me think that the Bible might not be the inerrant Word of God. For me, the Bible is perfect: it is just the thing that my wise and mighty heavenly Father knew I needed, and, when I read it, I see within it all the marks of its being his creation. Because of the illumination of the Holy Spirit, I hear God's voice in the Bible and recognize in my heart that this Word is truly God's Word being spoken to me. Because I trust him, I trust that there is not a single part of the Bible which would ever lead me away from the truth, even as I recognize the spiritual value in the disciplined hermeneutical work—and *team*work with my brother and sister Christians—that it often takes to rightly interpret what the Bible is claiming and communicating in each particular passage.

And so, although I am quite keenly aware that my explanation is inadequate, at the least I hope that it is equally inadequate to those on all sides of the conversation. For myself, if anything, I wish that in the midst of it all I could more clearly express how deeply and firmly I believe that all of the Bible is the true craftsmanship of God—all the facts, all the details—and that I trust every part of it without hesitation. I *love* the Bible. I believe the Bible, believe with all my heart that it represents God's real self-communication to his Church and to me as a part of it. I will never stop being thankful to God for the Bible: his own clear and true Word. I know that some people really feel that the 'problems' of Scripture are insurmountable, and I am always ready to honor the honesty of feeling that stands behind that position. But in my own life, when I look at them academically, or proportionally, I find the 'problems' to be pretty small, and in many cases (like variation in the manuscripts) not really problems at all, especially when I remember that the Bible genuinely is God's book, created according to his design and measured against the perfection of his own perfect will. It is impossible for me to think that the Bible is a bit of a failure for God, or doesn't really say things the way he wished they would have been said. He is the Almighty: nothing can stand in the way of him accomplishing his will. The Bible is inerrant. The Bible has no errors. Every part of it is exactly how God designed it to be. The Bible is perfect. It's just the Bible God wanted us to have.

### *If I was preparing for accreditation I would . . .*

- Be ready to talk about how I would respond to criticism of the Bible
- Make sure I understood the meaning of the terms 'inerrancy' and 'infallibility', and that our position on Scripture in the Alliance is that the Bible is 'inerrant'
- Read the first and last chapters of Peter Enns' book *Inspiration and Incarnation*
- Memorize Hebrews 1:1-2 and John 5:39

# 19. Missions

## *Why should the local church be involved in world missions?*

**"How can they hear about him unless someone tells them?" (Ro 10:14)**

Involvement in missions by the local church is important because of who God himself is. Missions is important because God is love. Remember: God's love is not something that simply characterizes him like a deeply ingrained habit, it runs much deeper than that; loving is not something that God *does*, it's *who he is*. The very existence of Father and Son, not just their relationship together, is rooted in the decision of God to love. God's will—the blueprint of his *being* and his actions—is a 'will-to-love'. God *is* the Father who loves the Son, and whose love overflows to us in creation. God *is* love. And so, God loves the lost, just as he loves you and me, and grieves at their absence from his family the Church. Moreover, in Christ he proved that he is prepared to do whatever it takes to bring them safely home. God's heart aches with affection and longing for the lost like a parent with a missing child. God's heart is a missionary heart. Missions is important because God loves the lost.

George Pardington said that "it cannot be too strongly emphasized that the Christian life is a Christ-life. It is not an imitation, but an incarnation. We do not copy Christ, we reproduce Him; or, rather, he reproduces His own life within us by the indwelling of the Holy Ghost." Being a Christian means having the life of God, having his 'will-to-love', reproduced in our own lives. And the place where this transformation takes place is the local church. Not the local church *building*, although that too may be an important place in our spiritual journey, but in and through the mutual fellowship of our brother and sister Christians in whatever context where God has placed us. The local church is where we hear and speak the Word of God one to another, where God meets us in the sacraments and in worship together, and where we are spiritually encouraged and are encouragers. The local church is the location of the sanctifying work of the Holy Spirit in our lives; it's the place where God makes us into people that love like he loves. Paul says that "we know how dearly God loves us, because he has given us the Holy Spirit to fill our hearts with his love." (Ro 5:5) Through the ordinary experience of celebrating life together in the local church, God fills our hearts with *his* kind of love. He pours it into our hearts until *we* grieve for the lost and ache for them to come safely home to God, until *our* experience of him is so rich and full of blessing that we are distracted by thinking about the things we could do to let *our* love—the love he himself has planted in us—overflow, and until *we* are prepared to do whatever it takes to extend his offer of salvation and forgiveness. Missions only really happens in that kind of context, when Christ's life is reproduced in the heart of Christian men and women by the indwelling presence of the Holy Spirit. The deeper life—the love-life of God reproduced in us—always comes before missions. First comes love.

Missions, then, is an important part of local church life because the local church is the community where all that transformation takes place, where God pours his life of love into our hearts and recreates our wills in the image of his 'will-to-love'. The local church is the place—the only place—where people who have had God's own missionary heart reproduced in them can be found. And so if the local church doesn't participate in missions, no one will. Romans explicitly speaks of this by asking about the lost: "How can they believe in him if they have never heard about him? And how can they hear about him unless someone tells them? And how will anyone go and tell them without being sent?" (Ro 10:14-15) The local church must witness, must be involved in missions, because missions is one of the great purposes for which God has designed it. "*You* will be my witnesses," commands Jesus, "telling people about me everywhere." (Ac 1:8) Not another, bigger, church, or some organization expressly set up for the work of missions: you.

And of course that doesn't mean we all *go*. We all know that there are lots of ways to be involved. Remember: when God's love overflowed to rescue us, the Father sent, the Son went, and the Spirit offered his special care and presence. And to say that 'missions includes the city where you are living just as much as the ends of the earth' is so clearly true that it is almost trite to say. The important thing is that the same heart motivates all of our involvement, whatever shape it takes. Not guilt or social pressure, not even duty, but a heart that has been changed by God so that it has genuinely begun to care about lost people, and is lodged in a life in which God has been slowly working so that its owner has begun to see how profound God's rescue really has been for them. Only a changed heart truly has something to offer; Christian missions is not the spread of 'Christianity' as an idea, but of Jesus Christ himself shining out through the living witness of sanctified believers.

Missionaries, and all the others who send and support them, are just ordinary people from local churches like yours and mine whose hearts God has transformed by his love. Nobody has the message of God's great salvation in the world except people like you and me from the local church. The local church is the community where God has been changing me into his image, and giving me his kind of love, and so my local church is the place where missions starts, and that's why it's important that my local church never stops wanting to be involved. A local church whose care and attention doesn't spill out in the direction of the lost, in one way or another, is ultimately an unhealthy church. It has lost its vital connection with the indwelling love of God the Holy Spirit. You see, God cares about the lost, and wants to reach out to them in love, and so he puts that love—his love—into the hearts of the everyday folk who live and pray and sing and clean and eat and chat and worship and give in the context of local church life. The local church is God's plan for missions, and the deeper life is his strategy for preparing us to take part.

## "Everyone will hate you because you are my followers." (Lk 21:17)

When I was a kid, nobody ever tried to stab my dad because he was a pastor. He's told us kids a few stories about some of the hard things he and my mom had to go through, but our house was never burned down, neither was our church, and no one ever staged a riot to shut down our services or chase us out of the neighborhood. In the West, for the most part, our Christian lives are protected from that kind of violence. That doesn't mean that Western pastors and congregations do not have endure all manner of more quiet persecutions, but we can thank God that our families are mostly safe from the threat of violence and our livelihoods are vulnerable only in the ways that everyone else's are.

In the rest of the world, the story is often different. In the rest of the world, there are still many places where angry people shake their fists at God in tangible ways, where they capture and kill his children, and where they burn and riot against meetings held in his name. But, somehow, this too is a part of God's plan, and participating in missions means being willing to allow some of our members, some of the brothers and sisters from our small group and from our local congregation, to leave their safer life and go to a place where being a Christian is much more difficult. We do it because, for us and them both, God's love overflows from within us through the Holy Spirit.

World missions is important because being the Church means standing in the center of the garden as the real body of Christ and being ready to take the rejection of the world. And our experience teaches us that this willingness to be exposed to rejection and hostility—like our Lord and savior Jesus Christ was—is the reality of local evangelism just as often as it is of international missions. It's what Jesus prepared his disciples for when he told them "everyone will hate you because you are my followers." (Lk 21:17) Because God's love is real love, a love that can be declined, God's plan for the world includes both the offer of salvation and the willingness to have that offer rejected. The Church, made strong by the Holy Spirit, fulfills both roles.

In a significant sense, missions is martyrdom; it's true self sacrifice. For the missionary it is the abandonment of home and career and friends and family and often the joy of one's own language to witness to the kindness of God in a new and often uncomfortable—and unreceptive—place. For the church that sends them it means the strain of care and the loss that comes with the separation of a meaningful part of the body. It is part of what missions giving is, a participation in the sacrifice that we as a body make together, and ready ourselves to make, so that we can both present God's great invitation and at the same time open ourselves up to the world's dismissal of it. In the history of our own church, the Alliance, being involved in missions has many times meant facing, or seeing loved ones face, physical harm, imprisonment, and death. We never seek these kinds of troubles, and we pray for God's protection from them, but we ready ourselves to encounter them. God has promised that he always loves us and that we never stand outside his providential care, but as the local church, because we really are the body of Christ, missions means extending ourselves out into the part of the world still hostile to Jesus Christ both in witness and in willingness to be rejected. That's what real love looks like.

In this regard, missions is a success even when all we do is simply determine to live in a place that hates our beloved Jesus. Sometimes victory just means deciding to stay on and withstand the dark spiritual and sometimes physical attack that constantly leans against us as the world and the spirit of the world rages and presses back against the presence of the body of Christ. Friend: if you are a local church member, pray God's strength for your friends in missions. We all yearn to see lost people come safely home to God, but missions is worthwhile even if there are never *any* converts, because a significant part of missions is the willingness of my own local church to tangibly offer the love of God, real love, in a way that can be rejected. Missions is the proof of the continuing truth of the love of God for the world. Evangelism, then, sometimes simply means stretching out as a church until we reach the place where the world is looking for a way to shout down God's gentle offer of salvation. The local church can never close itself off, it needs to extend itself until it can be seen in the middle of the garden, offering God's forgiveness in Jesus Christ and being ready to receive both the 'no!' and the 'yes!' of the world. Praise God that the 'yes!' is often heard. But yet we also need to remember that missions work, at home or abroad, means being willing to stand even in the face of a cruel 'no!', a 'no!' doubly painful for us because it makes us see how dark and lost life apart from Christ really is. Missions is important because the local church really is the body of Christ, and the body of Christ must allow itself to be the place where the world has an easy chance to reject God's offer of love.

Why is world missions important? It is important because we love Jesus. We go because he commands it, but much more so because he went, in person, to communicate this message. Missions is important for the local church because we really are God's plan to tell the story of his Good News—

we really are his witnesses—and because we really are the body of Christ.

### *If I was preparing for accreditation I would . . .*

- Read A. B. Simpson's sermon, "Enlarged Work," in *A Larger Christian Life*, chapter eleven
- Memorize Romans 10:14-15 and Matthew 24:14
- Start praying for one of my unbelieving friends or neighbors, and ask God to give me the opportunity to share his Good News with that friend

# 20. Christ our Coming King

*What are your expectations*
*regarding the return of Christ?*

Sadly, talking about what we expect will happen when Christ returns is often one of the easiest ways to start a quarrel in our churches. The felt distance between us, even as brother and sister Christians, can be immense, and is often compounded by how deeply we hold our opinions. Sometimes the result of this is that we, as pastors or teachers, try to avoid talking about the end times altogether, or teach about it only descriptively, merely explaining and laying out the main evangelical positions on issues like the millennium, the rapture, hell, or the number 666. (The technical term for this discussion about all the things related to what is going to happen when Christ comes back is 'eschatology'.) We just push it to the side in the interest of Christian unity. Less often, but more harmfully, some church leaders or Christian writers present just one position—or one narrow range of options—as the only 'true' choice, and then reject or belittle those in alternate camps as (usually) either unfaithful to Scripture or insensitive to culture, context, and community.

But of course both of these options are inadequate. We cannot stop talking and teaching about Christ's return, and we must not allow ourselves to promote division in the Church on account of it. How then can we move forward?

The first step is to admit that we don't know everything,

or even close to everything, about what is going to happen when Jesus comes back. For although the Bible has a lot to say about the end of the age, most of the details that it gives are difficult to interpret precisely. This is especially true in the cases where the Bible uses 'apocalyptic' language—the highly symbolic style of writing that communicates through the use of significant imagery such as beasts, scrolls, statues, horns, horses, special numbers, and the like. The 'apocalyptic' style of writing was reasonably common at the time when the Bible was written, but because we do not usually use it in our modern context we lack reference points to help us understand what all the symbols and images mean. It's a little like reading *Tristram Shandy* or *A Hundred Years of Solitude* if all we have ever been exposed to are traditional novels and the newspaper: fascinating, but difficult.

We ought therefore to avoid overconfidence in our abilities regarding some of the details, but that should never make us shy away from teaching and talking about Christ's return, about eschatology.

Mostly because figuring out how to get all these details right is not eschatology.

Of course, throughout our history as a church, so much energy has gone into discussing the details—things like the timing of the great tribulation or the meaning of this or that horn—that the average Christian can be excused for thinking that learning the right position on these issues is what it means to 'have a good eschatology'. But that's not true. Not that the details are abjectly uninterpretable or unimportant, not at all, just that they are by far not the *most* important.

What eschatology really means is figuring out how to

get our lives right in the present on account of the fact that Christ is coming again.

Eschatology is one of the areas of Christian theology that is most helped by thinking about it as a 'box', limited by several 'boundaries' or 'walls' that we do not allow ourselves to cross. The boundaries are not the eschatology itself, they are the limits that define the places that are safe for you and me when we try to understand life and the world in light of our hope in the second coming of Christ. Who am I before God? What is my responsibility to my neighbors? What is my life about? How should I live in this context where God has placed me? These are the real questions of eschatology, and they are questions that we answer inside the box.

It's a big box, like a great open prairie waiting for us pioneers to mark out our territories, but because we want to be true to the Bible and to each other we also acknowledge that it has its limits. We cannot go just anywhere we like, but there is enough room for me, along with my brother and sister Christians, to each have our own space—either close together or far apart—without feeling forced to all stand in exactly the same spot. Being faithful to Scripture here doesn't mean being identical, it means being diligent in not trespassing our boundaries; being sensitive to our community here doesn't mean walling ourselves off from one another, it means allowing each other to be somewhere else within our common limits, even when that particular 'somewhere else' feels strange and unusual. Most of all, for the pastor, it means having convictions about the best place to be 'inside the box'—we ought to be able to clearly and charitably express our own positions—but being able to contain some of the enthusiasm we have about our own great location and centering our teaching on the four great eschatological themes that make up the boundaries of the box.

## Jesus Christ really is coming again

The first and most important boundary of Christian eschatology is that Jesus Christ really is coming back, and coming as the undisputed King of the universe. In 1 Thessalonians, probably the very first book of the New Testament to be written, Paul states that "the Lord himself will come down from heaven with a commanding shout, with the voice of the archangel, and with the trumpet call of God. First, the Christians who have died will rise from their graves. Then, together with them, we who are still alive and remain on the earth will be caught up in the clouds to meet the Lord in the air. Then we will be with the Lord forever." (1Th 4:16-17) In more personal tones, Christ himself encourages his disciples that "there is more than enough room in my Father's home. If this were not so, would I have told you that I am going to prepare a place for you? When everything is ready, I will come and get you, so that you will always be with me where I am." (Jn 14:2-3) The return of Christ is real: we really will be caught up to meet him in the air, the dead really will be resurrected back to life, and Jesus really will gather up the sheep who know his voice and bring us safely home to God.

Jesus really is coming back. His return is not a metaphor for the progress of society or the accumulated impact of his teaching. He will return literally—tangibly—clothed with his glorious, perfected body to raise and perfect our bodies. It's the confession that stands at the very center of our faith: 'Christ has died, Christ has risen, Christ is coming again!' Maybe it's the most important and most true thing we ever really can say. Surely it is something that us brothers and sisters, as different as we are, can all celebrate together and guard as a limit of Christian thought and practice. There is a lot of space in the Church for eschatology, a lot of space to try and figure out how life ought to look in the light of the resurrection, but we can never transgress this boundary: Jesus Christ is coming again, as king, to claim and perfect his bride the Church, so that those who love him will be with him forever.

### Heaven and hell are real

The second boundary of eschatology is the reality of heaven and hell. I want to say this as carefully as I can so that I am not misunderstood: heaven is real, and hell is real, but, so long as we remain 'inside the box', it is not mandatory that we should all imagine heaven and hell in exactly the same way. At present, of course, there is a serious crisis in the evangelical church over heaven and hell, especially hell. The Bible itself describes hell in a number of ways. Probably some of the Bible's description of hell is figurative, meaning it tells the truth of the matter through illustrations rather than exact depictions. And certainly a fair portion of the pitch-fork-holding-devil kind of Christian mythology about hell that has grown up in the last two thousand years is simply mistaken. But, conversely, probably some of the Bible's description of hell is quite literal. Hell is real, and it is beyond our ability to imagine in its pain and horror. It comes as the consequence of the judgment of God on those who have rejected the salvation of his Son Jesus and have opposed his plan, and it is something that the Bible itself does not define the limit of. It is not necessarily hot or fiery, it is not even necessarily a 'place' in the way that we usually understand that word, but it is bad beyond any bad we can imagine, and some people genuinely will experience it. Historically, the Church has described it as 'eternal separation from God'. Hell is not a metaphor or a way of talking about the effects of sin in the world as we know it: hell is real.

Likewise, heaven is real, and it is physical, in a glorified sense of the word 'physical'. It is eternity with God, enjoying his and one another's company, and living interesting lives in a place that God himself has created expressly for our flourishing. Heaven too is the consequence of the judgment of God, grounded in the sacrifice of Christ, and by his grace it too is the destiny of a portion of humanity. It is good beyond anything we can imagine good to be. Heaven is real.

Within certain limits—inside the box—we can safely talk about this horribly bad place, and this wonderfully good place, that together represent the destiny of all humanity. What are they actually like? What is this or that passage of Scripture referring to when it talks about them? How does our understanding of the character of God affect the way that we think about them? We can ask all these kinds of questions about heaven and hell, and we don't even always have to agree on the answers, but we cannot ever deny their reality. Remember: "we must all stand before Christ to be judged. We will each receive whatever we deserve for the good or evil we have done in this earthly body." (2Co 5:10) Heaven and hell are real.

## Other People are important

The third boundary of Christian eschatology is the importance of people other than ourselves. This boundary has two key indicators. The first is, as Dwight Moody and others have said, that we should never be able to preach about hell without tears in our eyes. If hell is as horrible as we consider it to be, even just the thought of it should make us grieve. The lostness of some of our neighbors should never even begin to make us feel satisfied, or glad to see that someone who has disagreed with us or done us wrong will finally be receiving their just deserts. If it does, it means that our eschatology has gone far astray. Instead, the reality of the coming judgment of God ought to cause us to organize our lives to reflect just how important other people are and what an emergency life really is. Our expectation of the second coming should be the thing that amplifies our concern for our neighbors and causes us to reach out to them with love and forgiveness, never the opposite, because all people, especially the lost, are important to God.

The second indicator of this boundary is that other Christians are important too, even if their expectations about Christ's return seem bizarre to us, or maybe come across as going too far in accommodating culture. If our own opinions about the second coming are so narrow that we end up uncharitably cutting off fellowship with them, or looking down our noses at their naivete or their worldliness, then it is ultimately we and not they who are in the wrong. Remember: eschatology means figuring life out in light of the resurrection. That includes figuring out how to live in the Church—including the local church that you and I attend—with all the other Christians we find there, even when that is sometimes the most difficult bit. If our eschatology prevents us from getting along—or gives us a self-satisfied feeling of being right instead of sorrow at the fate of the lost—then it has crossed out of the 'box'. The freedom we have to think through and express our eschatology is limited because other people are important.

## The future always impacts the present

The fourth and final boundary of eschatology is the fact that, for the Christian, the future always impacts the present. If Jesus is coming, we need to be ready for him! The promise of the resurrection gives me hope, and helps me to make sense out of all the great difficulties that I see in the world around me, but it also actually affects the way that I live. It means caring about the people, even the difficult people, that God has put in my life in the way that God himself cares about them. It means learning to forgive, and to bless and not curse. It means obedience, and doing things God's way. It means providing for the physical needs of my neighbors as a way of expressing God's ongoing love for them. It means being responsible for all the things that God has given me— and for the planet on which he has placed me—as one who is going to have to give an account of how I used my life and all my advantages. It means all these things. Because God is unwilling to bring his kingdom in its fullness until all his children are accounted for, my hope in the return of Christ means that I support Christian missions to the world, especially to those peoples and communities who have no access to the gospel (which is a lesson I learned from A. B. Simpson and his use of Matthew 24:14, and which at first I really thought was bizarre, but have come to think that maybe he was right and I was wrong).

Most of all, because I already have God's deposit of the resurrection age in my heart, the Holy Spirit, my future life forever with God in heaven means that my present life is possible: it is possible to obey, it is possible to truly love my family, and my neighbor, it is possible to be patient even in suffering, it is possible to keep trusting even when I don't understand everything, and it is possible to live my life in a new kind of way. For us Christians, the future isn't just something that we will one day get to experience or, worse, something that ends up painting the present as the ultimately unmeaningful part of life. It is the opposite of that: it's something that has already begun arriving and is already making its presence felt right now. Christian eschatology means learning to live right now, but also, different from everyone else, living as if the future is just as real as the present. Because it is. Christian eschatology is never just about the future because, for the Christian, the future always impacts the present.

### *If I was preparing for accreditation I would...*

- Read Paul Spilsbury's book, *The Throne, the Lamb, and the Dragon*
- Memorize John 14:2-3 and 1 Thessalonians 4:16-17
- Be ready to discuss what I believe will happen when Christ comes back, and how that 'fits inside the box'
- Be aware that the word '*parousia*' is sometimes used as a technical term to talk about the arrival of the coming kingdom of God

# Appendix

## *Eight books every pastor should own*

When we first moved to Indonesia, we only brought what we could carry along with us on the plane. As a result, my personal library went down from around a thousand volumes to about a dozen. The books on this list are among the ones I brought, and I would gladly pay for them again if they were lost. These are books that have helped to shape my life—both as a Christian and a theologian—and ones I would recommend to anyone who was beginning in ministry (in addition to the recommended reading included at the end of the preceding chapters).

*The Christian Mind* by Harry Blamires
*Diary of Private Prayer* by John Baillie
*Exegetical Fallacies* by Don Carson
*A Message to Catholics and Protestants* by Oscar Cullmann
*The Mind of Christ* by Dennis Kinlaw
*The Offering of Man* by Harry Blamires
*Power through Prayer* by E. M. Bounds (the older title is
    *Preacher and Prayer*)
*A Tale of Three Kings* by Gene Edwards

# Glossary
(chapter numbers in parenthesis)

**Apocalyptic** — a highly symbolic style writing that was current at the time of the writing of the New (and the later parts of the Old) Testament; examples are Revelation and Daniel 7-13, along with many other non-biblical writings from the same time period like 'The Shepherd of Hermas' (20)

**Apollinarianism** — a form of Monophysitism, the heretical doctrine that in the incarnation God the Son took on the 'lower' elements of human nature, like flesh, but not a human mind or soul, which Apollinarius held was provided by his divine nature (8)

**atonement** — the act by which God, in Christ, overcame the problem of Sin that stood between himself and humanity, especially referring to the death of Jesus Christ on the cross and his resurrection (9)

**autographs** — a technical term referring to the original copies of the Bible, the ones that were first written down before they were copied or translated (17, 18)

**begotten** — the term used to describe the relationship that God the Son has to the Father, his life is grounded in the life of the Father, but he is himself a full divine Person equal to the Father; he is not a creation or the Father's offspring in a human sort of way (2)

**christology** — the technical term for the study of Jesus Christ, both as the eternal second Person of the Trinity and in his incarnation (8)

**Docetism** — the heretical doctrine that Jesus Christ only 'seemed to be' human, but was really only divine, that is, that Christ did not in truth possess a genuinely human nature but only appeared to do so; compare 'Valentinianism' (8)

**Donatist controversy** — the struggle in the Church to determine that the power of the sacraments, especially baptism, comes from God himself through the sacrament itself, and does not depend on the person who officiates the sacrament (15)

**Ebionitism** — a heresy rooted in Judaism that accepted Jesus as the Messiah but rejected his divinity; significantly parallel to Islam's acceptance of Jesus as 'al Masih', that is, 'the Messiah', but not as divine or the Son of God; this term is also used to talk about theological ideas that fail to take the physical aspect of our experience seriously (8)

**ecclesiology** — the technical term for the study of the Church (14)

**Eutychianism** — a form of Monophysitism, the heretical doctrine that Jesus Christ's human and divine nature were mixed together in the incarnation to form a 'third thing', that is, a new kind of nature neither wholly human nor wholly divine (8)

**eschatology** — the technical term for the conversation about the return of Christ and all the issues connected with it, which is also often used to talk about the way that the 'end times' have already begun to arrive and impact our lives in the present (20)

**Eucharist** — a term for communion, often used in more formal or more traditional church contexts, it's root meaning is 'to give thanks' (15)

**ex nihilo** — 'out of nothing'; a word used to describe God's way of creating, without needed any pre-existing materials and free from any outside influences (5)

**existentialism** — the philosophical position that understands life simply as the brute fact of existence, and that emphasizes that we only really begin to live when we take this life that we did not choose and decide to live it as our own (16)

**fall** — the moment in human history when Adam and Eve chose to reject God's plan and instead design their own, resulting in expulsion from the garden, slavery to Sin, and the cursing of the natural world (7)

**Gnosticism** — the mystical idea that the universe essentially consists in the struggle between a good force and an evil force; Gnosticism also conceives of the body and of physical things as essentially bad and of the spiritual as essentially good; liberation from the physical (bad) comes by way of secret knowledge (called 'gnosis') (8)

**grace** — the blessing and favor that God puts in our lives even though we don't deserve it (10)

**hamartiology** — the technical term for the study of Sin (7)

**homoousios** — a Greek word for describing the fact that Jesus is 'of the very same substance' as the Father (8)

**hypostasis** — the Greek word for Person in the context of the Trinity (2)

**hypostatic union** — union through being joined together in one Person; a very important theological term for describing how the eternal Son of God became a human; it means that Jesus Christ, the incarnate Son of God genuinely possesses two real natures, divine and human, which are permanently united in his one Person (hypostasis) without either being diminished or the two being in any way mixed up or muddled together (8)

**illumination** — the doctrine that the Holy Spirit helps earnest readers interpret the Scriptures by shining the light of his presence upon them as they read and study, and pointing out truth and error in their own thoughts; without the illumination of the Holy Spirit, accurately reading and understanding the Bible is impossible (17)

**image of God** — a phrase used to describe the way that humanity has been created by God in a special way so that we resemble him in several important ways, preeminently through our ability to love and to receive love (6)

**imago Dei** — the Latin phrase for the image of God (6)

**inerrant** — the evangelical doctrine that the Bible makes no errors in saying the things that it intends to say (18)

**infallible** — the doctrine that the Bible never leads us astray, especially regarding everything connected to God's self-revelation and to our salvation (18)

**incarnation** — the act of God the Son to take on human flesh ('carn' in the word incarnation means 'flesh', just like 'carn' in carnivore) and become a full human being, with a real human body and a real human nature, just like ours (8)

**inspiration** — the principle that God himself is the ultimate author of Scripture who directed and used human authors to communicate his true self (17)

**justification** — the act of God himself by which we are made right with God through Christ (10)

**lostness** — a word used in expressing the reality that, except through Jesus Christ, every person in the world lives under the dominion of Sin and is destined for eternal death; see also 'original sin' (7)

**missiology** — a very broad term used to refer to issues specifically related to Christian missions, including issues such as cross-cultural evangelism, anthropology, religious studies, etc (19)

**Modalism/Sabellianism** — a serious heresy regarding the nature of God, stating that God is only one Person (not three) but has three 'modes' or 'ways' of appearing in human history; present today in 'Oneness' or 'Jesus only' Pentecostalism; see also 'Patripassianism' (6)

**Monophysitism** — the heretical doctrine that Jesus Christ only had one nature, with either his human nature being swallowed up by his divine nature (Apollinarianism) or the two natures being fused together in his Person to make for a new mixed kind of nature (Eutychianism) (8)

**Monothelitism** — the heretical doctrine that Jesus had two natures, but only one will, that is, he possessed a divine will and not a human one (8)

**Nestorianism** — the heretical doctrine that, broadly speaking, Jesus Christ was two persons in addition to possessing two natures, that is, that his divine nature was not truly united with his human nature in one Person (8)

**omnipotence** — God's unlimited ability to accomplish what he wills to do, never lacking power; almightiness (4)

**omnipresence** — the term describing that God is always

present, in both space and time, especially to his creation (4)

**omniscience** — God's full knowledge and understanding of everything; not a logical puzzle, but a way of saying that God always knows: past, present, and future (4)

**ordo salutis** — the Latin phrase for 'the process of salvation' (10)

**original sin** — a term describing the way that the sin of Adam and Eve has had an effect on the whole of creation, including every human being; original sin means that we are not born totally free, but under the dominion of Sin: each of us has inherited a broken world and a broken self because of the sinfulness of Adam and Eve; see also 'lostness' (7)

**ousia** — the Greek word for substance in the context of the Trinity (2)

**parousia** — the technical term for arrival of the coming kingdom of God (20)

**Patripassianism** — the heretical idea that it was the Father who became human and suffered and died on the cross; see also Modalism/Sabellianism (6)

**Pelagianism** — the heretical doctrine that human beings can live free from sin even without the help of God's grace, empowered only by their own free will; (the ability of a Christian person to live in victory over sin through complete reliance on the power of the Holy Spirit is not Pelagianism, but the Christian doctrine of sanctification) (7)

**perichoresis** — a word describing the love of Father, Son, and Spirit; it means that each one is present in the life of the others in a maximally real way, that each one actually contributes to the being of the others; God's perichoretic unity means that we can never consider Father, Son, and Spirit alone, because in their love together they are one God (2)

**Person** — the word that best describes the Father, Son, and Spirit, when we consider them individually; God has shown himself to be three Persons, each possessing the characteristics of personhood and not as three 'powers' or 'forces' (2)

**plenary inspiration** — a technical term meaning that all the parts of the Bible are inspired by God, not just some of them (17, 18)

**pneumatology** — the technical term for the study of the Holy Spirit (12)

**Pneumatomacheanism** — a great technical term with which to impress your friends which means 'fighter against the Spirit', Peneumatomacheanism is the heresy of denying true divinity to the Holy Spirit, instead treating him as the created servant of Father and Son; strongly parallel to Arianism (8, 12)

**prevenient grace** — the grace of God that 'comes before' salvation which gives us both the inclination and the ability to return to God in repentance and faith (10)

**proceeds** — the word describing the relationship that God the Spirit has to the Father (and the Son); his life is grounded in theirs, but he is still a full Person himself, totally equal to Father and Son (2)

**proleptic** — a word describing how the effect of Jesus' sacrifice on the cross extends 'in both directions', including the people who came before him just as much as the people who come after him (9, 15)

**prosperity gospel** — the (erroneous) theological idea that Christianity is a way to escape from suffering and enjoy a materially better life; the idea that being a faith-filled Christian ought always to make a person healthy, wealthy, and wise (16)

**regeneration** — the theological term for being 'born again' (10)

**sacrament** — a word referring to communion and baptism, a sacrament is a physical symbol that conveys God's grace and presence in a special way; it is instituted by Jesus Christ and given its power to make a difference in our lives by the Holy Spirit, not by how 'well' or how 'purely' we do it (15)

**Septuagint** — a translation of the Old Testament into Greek dating to before Jesus; widely used at the time of the New Testament; often abbreviated LXX (8)

**soteriology** — the technical term for the study of salvation (10)

**substance** — the word used to talk about the 'God-ness' of God; whatever it is that God is, we refer to this being by saying that God is one substance; see also 'ousia' (2)

**theodicy** — the technical term for the very broad philosophical and theological discussion which tries to explain how a good and powerful God could allow bad things to happen (16)

**theology proper** — a term that is used to refer to the study of God himself, especially in reference to the being and attributes of God (4)

**Valentinianism** — the Gnostic heresy that Jesus Christ received a 'special' or 'divine' humanity directly from heaven and only passed through Mary 'like water through a pipe', taking on no aspect of her humanity, that is, he did not possess a human nature like we do, one affected by the fall; this doctrine was revived among the early Anabaptists (8)

**verbal inspiration** — the technical term meaning that the very words of the Bible are inspired by God, though not necessarily directly dictated by him (17, 18)

# Notes and Acknowledgments

Without the kind and patient love of God, and his challenge and calling in my heart, none of this book would be possible. I am profoundly thankful to him for everything. One of his greatest gifts has been my wife Kari, who has cheered me on and stood by me even on the days when I was feeling totally overwhelmed—and loved me—during this little project and as we have traveled all around the world together these last twelve or so years. Thank-you Kari; I love you; you know that I'd be lost without you. A special thank-you also to everyone who wrote me an encouragement card or read some of the early drafts of the accreditation helps project, especially all my students. I am thankful to you and to God for you for helping me not quit. Finally, I would like to thank my teachers, from all along the way (including 5/6 boys Sunday school), who, with great patience, taught me about the God who loves us, sent his Son who died to save us, gave us the Bible and the Church so that we would know him, and sent his Spirit to be among us and to change us into his own image.

Besides the above, I would like to specifically acknowledge my indebtedness to the following sources:

### Chapter 1
I learned that "although we cannot corral God intellectually, we can know him," from Thomas Aquinas. See "We can Know God but not Comprehend Him," 26-35.

I am thankful to Steve Flick for teaching me that the 'reward' in Hebrews 11:6 is God himself.

### Chapter 2
"The Trinity is like a family, like Adam, Eve, and Abel . . ." Gregory of Nyssa, "On the Faith", *NPNF2*, v.338.

### Chapter 4

"Brunner calls this fundamental aspect of *who God is* his 'will-to-love' . . ." in his book *Our Faith*, chapter 3.

Nietzsche's concept that all of life is based on a 'will to power' can be seen in his *Thus Spoke Zarathustra* (1883) or *Beyond Good and Evil* (1886).

### Chapter 5

I am thankful to Bill Ury, and especially the book *Mutuality* by Mary Prokes which he made me read, for teaching me how "God's love is the kind of love that overflows . . ."

### Chapter 6

"Bernard of Clairvaux, the twelfth century French monk, wrote that the highest level of love, higher even than loving God for God's own sake, was learning to love yourself . . ." in *On Loving God*, book 10.

### Chapter 7

"Augustine reminds us that babies aren't any more sinless than anyone else . . ." in *The Confessions*, *I.vii.11*.

### Chapter 8

"Gregory of Nazianzus (one of my favorite theologians) said, 'that which He has not assumed He has not healed . . .'" in his first letter "To Cledonius the Priest Against Apollinarius," *NPNF2*, vii.440.

"George Pardington rightly says, Jesus Christ is the Yahweh of the Old Testament," in his book *Christian Doctrine*, 234.

"The Gospels are all thus unafraid to use name Yahweh to refer to Jesus. Quoting Isaiah 40:3 they present John the Baptist as the one preaching repentance . . . in what Kavin Rowe calls 'an indisputable citation from the Old Testament.' He writes that, in Luke and Acts, 'to speak of Yahweh is to speak of Jesus and vice versa.'"

Both Kavin Rowe quotations are from his remarkable paper "Luke and the Trinity," 18; I am tremendously grateful to have been given it by

Scot Becker when I was working through this theme; I would have never found on my own. Rowe's argument—that certain New Testament references to 'Jesus as Lord' contain clear and intentional quotations from the Old Testament where 'Lord' is used both as a Greek translation of the OT word YHWH as well as the *kere* in Hebrew reading—is the origin of this paragraph and a strong buttress of the following one (cf. his 25) which I had already written when I read his work. Rowe's paper, though probably inaccessible to the unprepared reader, is the very best I have read on the topic of New Testament references to Jesus as God and has significantly impacted my own thinking on the matter.

**Chapter 9**
"Thomas Oden reminds us in his book *The Word of Life*, being human means being particular . . ." in the second volume of his Systematic Theology, *The Word of Life*, 121-2.

The theme that Christ's victory over Sin, Death, and the Devil is one of the most important aspects of his death and resurrection owes its resurgence in the last century (and its inclusion here) in large part to the seminal book *Christus Victor* by Gustav Aulen.

**Chapter 10**
"Billy Graham, in one of the best and most straightforward books on salvation I have read, wrote about this . . ." in his book *Peace with God*, 143.

I am grateful for John Baillie's sermon "To Pray and Not Faint" which shaped my understanding of what it really means to pray, and what Jesus was communicating in Luke 18. It comes from Baillie's book, *Christian Devotion*, which remains one of my favorite short collections of sermons.

**Chapter 11**
"A. B. Simpson said, because 'sickness has come into the world through sin . . .'" in "Divine Healing in the Atonement." I am indebted for this quotation to the collection of Alliance resources *Readings in Alliance History and Thought* collected by Kenneth Draper.

I am grateful to my teachers in New Testament at Canadian Bible College, especially Andy Reimer and John Earnshaw, from whom I learned that "we live sort of caught in between, already in the kingdom, but not yet seeing its final manifestation;" this theme gained force in the evangelical church through G. E. Ladd's important book *A Theology of the New Testament*.

The theme that Christ's victory over Sin, Death, and the Devil is one of the most important aspects of his death and resurrection owes its resurgence in the last century (and its inclusion here) in large part to the seminal book *Christus Victor* by Gustav Aulen.

**Chapter 12**
"The Alliance position on speaking in tongues is 'expectation without agenda' . . ." Further reading on this topic can be found in Charles Nienkirchen's fantastic collection of early Alliance documents, *The Man, the Movement, and the Mission*, especially 168-205. Nienkirchen records the following quote on the gift of tongues from A. B. Simpson:

> The statement is made by unfriendly parties sometimes that the Alliance and its leaders are opposed to the manifestation of the Gift of Tongues in this age. This is wholly false. Our attitude has been often stated and is consistent and explicit. We fully recognize all the gifts of the Spirit, including 'diverse kinds of tongues' as belonging to the Church in every age. And many of our most wise and honored workers both in the homeland and in the mission field have had this experience. But we are opposed to the teaching that this special gift is for all or is the evidence of the Baptism of the Holy Ghost. . . . We give and we claim charity and liberty, that those who have not this experience shall recognize in the Lord those who have it and use it to edification. And that those who have it, shall equally recognize those who have not this special form of divine anointing. (173)

The Alliance position is an effort to avoid four pitfalls: (1) denying tongues as one of the normal kinds of things that can happen in the life of a Spirit-filled Christian, (2) demanding that tongues is a 'necessary sign', that is, if you haven't spoken in tongues you aren't really filled with the Spirit, (3) making the whole of the spiritual life all about speaking in tongues, and (4) allowing tongues to be an excuse for schism within the church, or to underlie a lack of charity between us, which is of course opposite to the kind of thing we ought to expect the Holy Spirit to accomplish in our lives.

## Chapter 13
The theme that Christ's victory over Sin, Death, and the Devil is one of the most important aspects of his death and resurrection owes its resurgence in the last century (and its inclusion here) in large part to the seminal book *Christus Victor* by Gustav Aulen.

"Gregory wrote that: This is true perfection . . ." in *The Life of Moses*, 137.

## Chapter 15
"We were not there when Christ was sacrificed for our sins, but when we eat the bread and drink the cup in faith God freely and graciously applies the offering of Christ afresh to each one of us." I first understood this parallel—between families in ancient Israel and the effect of communion for us even though we were not present at the sacrifice—by means of the work of B. B. Warfield.

"what Ignatius called the 'medicine of immortality . . .'" in his letter "To the Ephesians," *ANF*, i.58.

## Chapter 16
I am thankful for John Oswalt for teaching me that God never fails to see or care our sufferings, especially through his sermon on Psalm 56:8.

## Chapter 17
That " . . . reading in a foreign language forces you to go so slowly," is an insight I owe to John Oswalt.

## Chapter 18
I am grateful to Trevor Rysavy for first loaning me *Inspiration and Incarnation* and talking to me about its contents.

## Chapter 19

Pardington says that "it cannot be too strongly emphasized that the Christian life is a Christ-life . . ." in *Outline Studies in Christian Doctrine*, 323.

## Chapter 20

I am grateful to Paul Spilsbury and Gary Cockerill for (patiently) teaching me how to understand the writings of the New Testament according to their genre, and to Peter Baumann for *Tristram Shandy*.

The phrase "Christ has died, Christ has risen, Christ will come again" is a traditional affirmation of the Anglican and Methodistic churches.

The phrase 'eternal separation from God' can be found in the *Catechism of the Catholic Church*, paragraph 1035.

I am thankful to my friend E. M. who taught me the principle that Christian missions is "all about 'access to the gospel;'" I know the phrase is not original to him, but I never would have really been able to capture it like that in my own mind without his help.

—

# Bibliography

Aquinas, Thomas. "We can Know God but not Comprehend Him," in *Summa Theologiae: A Concise Translation*. Edited by Timothy Mc-Dermott. Westminter, MD: Christian Classics, 1989.

Augustine. *Confessions of St. Augustine*. Translated by E. B. Pusey. London: Thomas Nelson, nd. http://www.ccel.org/ccel/augustine/confess.html

Aulen, Gustav. *Christus Victor: An Historical Study of the Three Main Types of the Idea of Atonement*. Translated by A. G. Hebert. London: SPCK, 1931.

Baillie, John. *Christian Devotion*. New York: Charles Scribner's Sons, 1962. http://www.luc.edu/faculty/pmoser/idolanon/BaillieChristian-Devotion.html

Basil the Great. *On the Holy Spirit*. Crestwood, NY: St. Vladimir's Seminary Press, 1980. http://www.ccel.org/ccel/schaff/npnf208.vii.i.html

Bernard of Clairvaux. *On Loving God*. Christian Classics Etherial Library. http://www.ccel.org/ccel/bernard/loving_god.html

Blamires, Harry. The Offering of Man. New York: Morehouse-Barlow, 1960.

Brunner, Emil. *I Believe in the Living God: Sermons on the Apostles' Creed*. Translated by John Holden. Philadelphia: Westminster, 1956.

Brunner, Emil. *Our Faith*. Translated by John W. Rilling. London: SCM, 1949 (1936).

Carson, D. A. *Exegetical Fallacies*. Second edition. Grand Rapids: Baker Academic, 1996.

*Catechism of the Catholic Church*. New York: Image, 1995.

Cullmann, Oscar. *Message to Catholics and Protestants*. Translated by Joseph A. Burgess. Grand Rapids: Eerdmans, 1959.

Edwards, Gene. *A Tale of Three Kings: A Study in Brokenness*. Scarborough: Christian Books, 1980.

Enns, Peter. *Inspiration and Incarnation: Evangelicals and the Problem of the Old Testament*. Grand Rapids: Baker Academic, 2005.

Graham, Billy. *Peace with God*. Nashville: Thomas Nelson, 1953. http://www.gotothebible.com/HTML/peacewithGodtoc.html

Gregory of Nazianzus. "To Cledonius the Priest Against Apollinarius: Letter 101." In *Select Library of Nicene and Post-Nicene Fathers of the Christian Church, Second Series*. Edited by Philip Schaff. Fourteen volumes. Reprint, Peabody, MA: Hendrickson, 1999 (1890-1900). Volume VII. http://www.ccel.org/ccel/schaff/npnf207.iv.ii.iii.html

Gregory of Nyssa. *The Life of Moses*. Translated by Abraham J. Malherbe and Everett Ferguson. New York: Paulist, 1978.

Gregory of Nyssa. "On the Faith." In *Select Library of Nicene and Post-Nicene Fathers of the Christian Church, Second Series*. Edited by Philip Schaff. Fourteen volumes. Reprint, Peabody, MA: Hendrickson, 1999 (1890-1900). Volume V. http://www.ccel.org/ccel/schaff/npnf205.viii.vi.html

Ignatius of Antioch. "To the Ephesians." In *The Ante-Nicene Fathers: Translations of the writings of the Fathers down to AD 325*. Edited by Alexander Roberts and James Donaldson. Ten volumes. Reprint, Peabody, MA: Hendrickson, 1994 (1885-97). Volume I. http://www.ccel.org/ccel/schaff/anf01.v.ii.html

Keita, Isaac. "Person and Work of the Holy Spirit." http://www.awf.nu/en/Person-and-Work-of-the-Holy-Spirit

Ladd, George E. *A Theology of the New Testament*. Second edition. Edited by Donald A. Hagner. Grand Rapids: Eerdmans, 1993.

Lewis, C. S. *God in the Dock: Essays on Theology and Ethics*. Edited by Walter Hooper. Grand Rapids: Eerdmans, 1970.

*The Man, the Movement, and the Mission: A Documentary History of the Christian and Missionary Alliance*. Compiled by Charles Nienkirchen. Regina: Canadian Theological Seminary, 1987. http://www.cmalliance.org/resources/ archives/downloads/miscellaneous/man-movement-mission.pdf

Oden, Thomas. *Pastoral Theology: Essentials of Ministry*. New York: HarperCollins, 1983.

Oden, Thomas. *The Word of Life: Systematic Theology, Volume II*. San Francisco: Harper and Row, 1989.

Piper, John. *Filling Up the Afflictions of Christ*. Wheaton: Crossway, 2009. http://www.desiringgod.org/resource-library/online-books/ filling-up-the-afflictions-of-christ

Pardington, George. *Outline Studies in Christian Doctrine*. Camp Hill, PA: Christian Publications, 1926. http://baptistbiblebelievers.com/BookList/OUTLINESTUDIESINCHRISTIANDOCTRINESParding-ton/tabid/434/Default.aspx

Prokes, Mary Timothy. *Mutuality: The Human Image of Trinitarian Love. New York: Paulist, 1993.*

*Readings in Alliance History and Thought.* Selected and edited by Kenneth L. Draper. https://online.ambrose.edu/alliancestudies/ahtreadings/ahtr_con.html

Rowe, Kavin. "Luke and the Trinity: an essay in ecclesial biblical theology." *Scottish Journal of Theology* 56(1):1-26, 2003.

Simpson, Albert Benjamin. "Divine Healing in the Atonement." Christian and Missionary Alliance Weekly, (August 1890): 122-124. In *Readings in Alliance History and Thought.*

Simpson, Albert Benjamin. "Editorial: taken from *The Christian and Missionary Alliance.*" In *The Man, the Movement, and the Mission,* 173.

Simpson, Albert Benjamin. "Enlarged Work," in *A Larger Christian Life.* Camp Hill, PA: Christian Publications, 1988. Chapter 11. http://www.cmalliance.org/resources/archives/downloads/simpson/larger-christian-life.pdf

Spilsbury, Paul. *The Throne, the Lamb, and the Dragon.* Downers Grove: InterVarsity, 2002.

"Spiritual Gifts: Expectation without Agenda." Christian and Missionary Alliance. http://www.cmalliance.org/about/beliefs/perspectives/spiritual-gifts

# Index

156-8
Nero, 118
Nestorianism, 52, 164
Nicene Creed, 82
Nietzsche, 23, 170
normal, 46, 67, 72, 77, 79, 81, 89,
    118-20, 129, 172

Oden, Thomas, 57, 115, 171
omnipotence, 25, 29, 164
omnipresence, 164
omniscience, 20, 25-6, 29, 165
one-ness, 9-11, 13, 22
*ordo salutis*, 165
original sin, 42, 164-5
*ousia*, 6, 13, 104, 165, 167
overflowing love, 2, 15, 23, 29,
    32-4, 38-9, 122, 125, 142-3,
    146, 170

Palestine, 103
Pardington, George, 142, 170, 174
parents, 25, 33, 40, 42, 142
parousia, 158, 165
pastors, 21, 69, 71, 80, 100-2,
    106-7, 113, 117-8, 126, 132-3,
    145-6, 150, 152, 159
Patripassianism, 38, 164, 165
peace, 25, 55, 78, 121
Pelagianism, 42, 165
Pentecostalism, 89, 164
perfect, 10, 20, 27-8, 46, 67, 74,
    77, 86, 93, 101, 121, 137, 139,
    140-1, 153-4
perfected, 58, 73, 153
perfection, 28, 67, 96, 139-40,
    173
perichoresis, 10-1, 13, 165, 166

Person, 7-8, 10, 24, 33, 38, 48,
    52-4, 66, 83-5, 87, 89, 160,
    162, 163, 164, 166
personal, 3, 9, 12-3, 20, 26, 43,
    56, 81, 83-5, 89, 105, 114,
    138, 153, 159
personal relationship, 66, 67
philosophy, 21, 23-5, 116, 162
physical, 35, 36, 43, 71-5, 99,
    100-2, 105, 109-11, 113-4,
    147, 155, 157, 161-2, 167
Piper, John, 127
'plenary inspiration', 134, 166
pneumatology, 166
Pneumatomacheanism, 166
power, 2, 14, 18, 23, 27, 34, 44,
    48, 51, 53, 57-9, 62, 67, 71,
    76-8, 85, 87, 89-91, 93-4, 101,
    105, 113-4, 119, 122, 129,
    130, 133, 161, 164, 165, 167,
    170
prayer, 69, 72, 76, 78-81, 82, 100,
    107, 110-1, 145, 147-9, 171
preaching, 50, 58, 73, 88, 94, 106,
    111, 156, 170
pre-existent, 51
presence, 9, 28, 33, 45, 83, 86-7,
    89, 92, 99-100, 102, 104-5,
    113-4, 119, 139, 143-4, 148,
    158, 163, 167
prevenient grace, 62, 70, 166
proceeds, 12-3, 82, 166
process theology, 30
Prokes, Mary, 170
proleptic, 166
prosperity gospel, 119, 167
punishment, 56, 96

Trinity, 2, 5-19, 31, 51, 82, 84-5,
104, 111, 122, 160, 162, 165,
166, 169, 170
trust, 26, 27, 108, 126, 130, 136,
137, 139, 140
trustworthiness, 15, 26, 130-1,
137
truth, 14, 17, 43, 59, 65, 91, 102,
113, 129, 133, 136, 140, 148,
154, 161, 163

unbegotten, 12
uniqueness, 15-7, 57, 64, 66, 97,
129
united, 47, 52-4, 163, 164
unity, 10-1, 13, 16, 53, 102, 110,
150, 166

universal, 103-4

Valentinianism, 167
'verbal inspiration', 134, 168
victory, 24, 57-9, 60, 67-8, 75-7,
81, 90-2, 147, 165, 171, 172,
173

will-to-love, 23-5, 27, 32, 34, 113,
142-4
women, 15, 20, 32, 35, 47, 65-6,
72, 84, 92, 102, 137, 143, 169
worship, 13, 82, 85-6, 89, 100,
105, 109, 111-2, 114, 143, 145

Yahweh, 49-52, 54, 170-1